The Recruiting Officer

THE NEW MERMAIDS

General editor: Brian Gibbons
Professor of English Literature, University of Münster

THE NEW MERMAIDS

The Recruiting Officer

GEORGE FARQUHAR

Edited by

JOHN ROSS

Senior Lecturer in English
Massey University, New Zealand

LONDON/A & C BLACK

NEW YORK/W W NORTON

Second edition 1991
Reprinted 1992, 1995, 1996
Published by A & C Black (Publishers) Limited
35 Bedford Row, London WC1R 4JH
ISBN 0–7136–3349–2

© A & C Black (Publishers) Limited

First New Mermaid edition 1973
by Ernest Benn Limited
© 1973 Ernest Benn Limited

Published in the United States of America
by W. W. Norton & Company Inc.
500 Fifth Avenue, New York, N.Y. 10110

ISBN 0–393–90065–7

A CIP catalogue record for this book
is available from the British Library

Printed in Great Britain by
Whitstable Litho Printers Ltd,
Whitstable, Kent

CONTENTS

ACKNOWLEDGEMENTS

IN PREPARING THIS EDITION I have been greatly indebted to the work of previous editors, A. C. Ewald, William Archer, Louis B. Strauss, Charles Stonehill, Michael Shugrue, and A. Norman Jeffares, in treatment of the text, annotation, and critical comment. Eric Rothstein's and Eugene Nelson James's books on Farquhar have provided more critical insights than it is practical to acknowledge in detail. For training in the techniques of editing I am grateful to Professors Donald F. McKenzie and Harold F. Brooks. Help has been given generously in the later stages of the present task by Professor Roland Frean, Professor Brooks, Mrs Diana Gurney, Dr David Foxon, the National Army Museum, the English Folk Song Society, the reference librarians of the Alexander Turnbull and Massey University Libraries, and my wife Audrey.

I have appreciated very much the assistance of Miss Marianne Wheatley, in her careful typing of the manuscript.

Massey University   JOHN ROSS

ACKNOWLEDGEMENTS

LIST OF ABBREVIATIONS

Archer	Archer, William, ed., *George Farquhar [Best Plays]*, London, new edition, 1949
Ashton	Ashton, John, *Social Life in the Age of Queen Anne*, London, 1883 (facsimile edition, Detroit, Michigan, 1968)
C18	eighteenth century
Ed.	editorial emendation
Ewald	Ewald, Alexander Charles, ed., *The Dramatic Works of George Farquhar*, 2 vols., London, 1892
fig.	figuratively
Hunt	Hunt, Leigh, ed., *The Dramatic Works of Wycherley, Congreve, Vanbrugh and Farquhar*, London, 1840
James	James, Eugene Nelson, *The Development of George Farquhar as a Comic Dramatist*, The Hague, 1972
Jeffares	Jeffares, A. Norman, ed., *The Recruiting Officer* (Fountainwell Drama Texts), Edinburgh, 1972
The London Stage	W. van Lennep, E. L. Avery, A. H. Scouten, G. W. Stone and C. B. Hogan, edd., *The London Stage, 1660–1800*, 11 vols., Carbondale, Illinois, 1960–68
n.	note
N & Q	*Notes and Queries*
N.T.	National Theatre production, 1963
Nicoll	Nicoll, Allardyce, *A History of English Drama 1660–1900*, 6 vols., Vol. II, *Early Eighteenth Century Drama*, 3rd edition, Cambridge, 1955
Q	early editions
Q1	first edition, 1706
Q2	second edition, 1706
Rothstein	Rothstein, Eric, *George Farquhar*, New York, 1967
s.d.	stage direction
s.p.	speech prefix
Shugrue	Shugrue, Michael, ed., *The Recruiting Officer* (Regents Restoration Drama Series), London, 1966
Stonehill	Stonehill, Charles, ed., *The Complete Works of George Farquhar*, 2 vols., Bloomsbury, 1930
Strauss	Strauss, Louis B., ed., *A Discourse upon Comedy, The Recruiting Officer and The Beaux' Stratagem* (Belles-Lettres Series), Boston [1914]

Tilley   Tilley, Morris Palmer, *A Dictionary of the Proverbs in England in the Sixteenth and Seventeenth Centuries*, Ann Arbor, 1950

Tynan   Tynan, Kenneth, ed., '*The Recruiting Officer*': *The National Theatre Production*, London, 1965

INTRODUCTION

THE AUTHOR

THE CHANCES OF BIRTH firmly linked George Farquhar's life with soldiering, and with the latest phase of Restoration comedy. He entered the world in Londonderry in northern Ireland *ca.* 1677, and endured the 105 days' siege of that city in 1688–89.[1] During this time his father, an Anglican clergyman serving a nearby parish, was 'plundered and burnt out of all he had, and not long after dy'd with greif', leaving his son without means.[2] George is said to have taken some part as a young volunteer at the Battle of the Boyne in 1690. The Pindaric ode he wrote soon after 'On the Death of General Schomberg' in this struggle indicates the direction of his thinking about war, as sometimes necessary and honourable yet even in victory tragically costly for those involved.

From the Londonderry Grammar School George went on to Trinity College, Dublin, in 1694, probably intending to follow his father's profession. After two years, however, he gave up his studies, and a growing friendship with the actor Robert Wilks led to his joining the company at the Smock Alley theatre, managed by Joseph Ashbury. He proved to have too thin a voice and stage-presence to sustain major roles, despite Ashbury's expert instruction, and suffered from persistent stage-fright; yet he was well-liked, and had gained a year's invaluable practical experience when his career was cut short by a distressing accident. During a performance he was to stab a fellow-actor, but first to switch his sword for a foil. In his excitement he forgot to do so, inflicting a serious wound. Although the man recovered, Farquhar was so shaken that he gave up acting, and on Wilks's advice travelled to London to try his hand as a playwright.

His first comedy, *Love and a Bottle*, scored a modest success in 1698 and proved, as its title suggests, that its author had absorbed the stock topics, character-types, and situations of Restoration comedy well enough to employ them playfully. This same year saw the appearance of Jeremy Collier's *Short View of the Immorality and*

[1] The most reliable account of Farquhar's life is in Eric Rothstein's *George Farquhar* (New York, 1967), Chapter 1, where due weight is given to the imprecision or uncertainty of the available 'facts'.

[2] J. R. Sutherland, 'New Light on George Farquhar', *Times Literary Supplement,* 6 March 1937, p. 171, citing his widow's petition.

Profaneness of the English Stage which signalled the approaching withdrawal of the licence the dramatists had enjoyed to write to please their audiences without external moral censorship, and, also, a shift in the taste of those audiences towards sentimentalism. Sir Harry Wildair in Farquhar's next play, *The Constant Couple*, was probably the last of the gay extravagant libertine-rakes of the old kind. Opening in November 1699 with Wilks in the leading role, this play was phenomenally popular, making fortunes for other men, but not for its author. It helped, incidentally, to spoil the box-office for Congreve's last masterpiece, *The Way of the World*, at the rival theatre. After such a triumph the reception of his next efforts, *Sir Harry Wildair*, a pallid sequel, in 1701, *The Inconstant* (an adaptation of Fletcher's *Wild Goose Chase*) and *The Twin Rivals*, in 1702, proved sadly disappointing. A successful short farce, *The Stage-Coach*, adapted from Jean de la Chapelle's *Les Carosses d'Orléans*, is of interest as Farquhar's first use of a setting outside London and for its pioneering of some of the dramatic materials of *The Beaux' Stratagem*. Neither these plays nor his miscellaneous writings secured for their author patronage generous enough to make up for the humiliation of seeking it; and in 1703 he worsened his position by marrying a penniless widow with two children, seemingly in the belief that like a comedy hero he was marrying a wealthy heiress.

In 1701–02 the struggle between France and the Grand Alliance powers, Britain, the Dutch, and the Austro-German Empire, halted by treaty in 1697, had flared up once more as the War of the Spanish Succession. In 1704 the Earl of Orrery granted Farquhar a commission as Lieutenant of Grenadiers in his newly formed regiment of foot with a salary of £54 15s. a year, and assigned him to recruiting in the English midlands. So it was that at some time in 1705, after a period in Lichfield, he shifted his activities to Shrewsbury. That he was diligent appears from his colonel's testimony that he had been 'very Serviceable both in Raising and Recruteing ye sd. Reigmt. to ye great prejudice of his family', meaning presumably he had spent too much of his own money.[3] That he enjoyed his stay is evident in his dedication of *The Recruiting Officer* to all his friends in the area, who by their hospitality and loyalty 'made recruiting, which is the greatest fatigue upon earth to others, to be the greatest pleasure in the world to me'. While in Shrewsbury (reputedly in a certain room overlooking the yard in the Raven Inn) he wrote most at least of this comedy, probably working quickly in a burst of high spirits. By 12 February 1706 it was sufficiently complete for him to sell the publication rights to the bookseller Bernard Lintott for £16 2s. 6d.,

[3] ibid.

and on 8 April it opened at the Theatre Royal, Drury Lane. It became at once immensely popular, and would prove one of the most often revived plays of the century.

Farquhar none the less was soon deep in debt again and became gravely ill, probably with tuberculosis. A kindly visit to his London garret by Robert Wilks in mid-December stimulated him into working furiously on another comedy, *The Beaux' Stratagem*. Completed by the end of January and performed in April, it was brilliantly successful. About 20 May (he was buried on the 23rd) its author died, not more than thirty years old, leaving his family to sink into destitution.

A remark in *Love and a Bottle* that 'the Hero in Comedy is always the Poet's Character' has naturally encouraged critics to deduce Farquhar's own personality from those of his heroes, seeing him as gay, bubbling with vitality, rattle-brained, and whimsically resourceful. His '*Picture*' of himself in his miscellany *Love and Business* (1702) emphasized that 'Melancholy' was the 'every Day Apparel' of his mind, and it had 'hitherto found few Holydays to make it change its Cloaths'. His constitution was 'very Splenatick, and yet very Amorous. . .' He lacked, then, the deeper anxieties of responsibility for a family, and the ill-health of at least his last year of life. He also described here his capacity to work on his plays with extreme intensity for a short time. His 'Discourse upon Comedy' in the same miscellany demonstrates his concern with the nature of his craft. He defined comedy as a '*well-fram'd Tale handsomly told, as an agreeable Vehicle for Counsel or Reproof*'.[4] Form was needed, but it should be derived empirically from nature and from function, the requirements of the theatre and audience of the time, rather than from neoclassical rules. Eugene Nelson James in *The Development of George Farquhar as a Comic Dramatist* has ably demonstrated the corresponding presence in his middle plays, from 1701, of a search for adequate form, culminating in his two masterpieces. His artistic problems have been recognized by James as the achievement of coherence and unity with several plot-strands, the appropriate balancing of humour and wit, and the moulding of each play as an effective vehicle for a serious, original vision of life, without ceasing to amuse.

If in retrospect his last two plays appear to us as the last worthwhile comedies of the Restoration tradition, this is due partly at least to the historical accidents of Farquhar's own premature death, and of the failure of his successors to write works of comparable stature, until the emergence of Goldsmith and Sheridan some seventy years

---

[4] Stonehill, I, 51; II, 315–16, 336.

later. The significant trends in the theatres were towards Italianate opera, and the sentimental comedy mode inaugurated by Cibber and Steele. It is indicative of the pressures being exerted by the Reformers of Manners and by Queen Anne's Lord Chancellor against profanity and indecency that the attempted seductions in Farquhar's last plays are both frustrated of consummation. It is evident none the less that Farquhar was breaking new ground technically and extending the range of true comedy to suit his own talents, and the changing society and audiences of his time.

SOURCES

Farquhar's inexplicit comment in his dedicatory epistle that 'some little turns of humour that I met with almost within the shade of [the Wrekin] gave the rise to this comedy' may have stimulated the curiosity of Bishop Percy. He wrote to one E. Blakeway, in Shrewsbury, who replied on 4 July 1765 that he had consulted an old lady in the town:

> She says that she well remembers Farquhar on a recruiting party in this town, where he continued some time, long enough to write his Play. I do not think for my own part that the characters therein described have in them much of singularity, but you are in the right in believing that he had living originals in his eye. Her account of them is as follows:
> Justice Balance is M.ʳ Berkley then Deputy Recorder of the town – one of the other Justices a M.ʳ Hill an inhabitant of Shrews-bury. – M.ʳ Worthy is M.ʳ Owen of Rusason on the borders of Shropshire – Capt.ⁿ Plume is Farquhar himself – Brazen unknown. – Melinda is Miss Harnage of Belsadine near the Wrekin. – Silvia Miss Berkley Daughter of the Recorder above mentioned. – The story I suppose the Poet's invention.[5]

Farquhar had acknowledged in his epistle that Balance and Bullock were 'drawn . . . in their *puris naturalibus*' from living men.[6] Miss Berkley's first name was Laconia, making Brazen's calling Balance 'Mr Laconic' in Act III, scene i, a kind of private joke. There is, further, a tradition that Kite was modelled on Farquhar's assistant in recruiting, Sergeant Jones.

Blakeway has, however, chosen his words judiciously. Whatever

[5] From a copy interleaved in a British Museum copy of Giles Jacob, *The Poetical Register* (1720, 1719), I, between pp. 98 and 99.
[6] Other possible models for Balance and Silvia, Alderman Gosnell and his daughter, are given in Thomas Wilkes's biography in the 1775 Dublin edition of Farquhar's *Works*, I, x–xi.

resemblances these characters may have been given to 'living originals', they are primarily variations upon well-tried character types or formulae, firmly established in Restoration comedy, and used repeatedly and with increasing skill by Farquhar himself in his earlier plays, as James has demonstrated in *The Development of George Farquhar as a Comic Dramatist*. He has thereby provided a much-needed undermining of the over-simplistic assumptions of biographical critics. James's reaction even to the recruiting scenes, that area of the play where Farquhar would have drawn most closely upon observation of life and his own experiences, is not 'How realistic!' but 'Why isn't there more realism in the play?' (p. 225).

The answers lie first in the conservatism of the contemporary theatre audience, who, as Farquhar had complained, 'take all innovations for grievances . . . A play without a beau, cully, cuckold or coquette, is as poor an entertainment for some palates as their Sunday dinners would be without beef and pudding'.[7] And further, the natural, easy surface of the play, as I will argue in the critical section, conceals a considerable degree of artifice. Farquhar's use of the poet-character Lyric in *Love and a Bottle*, and his 'Discourse upon Comedy', reveal a dramatist very conscious of the largely artificial nature of contemporary comedy, which he could modify and even transcend but not ignore.

There are no specific literary sources, though Farquhar had a precedent for the court-room impressment scene, Act V, scene v, in Shakespeare's *2 Henry IV*, III.ii, and for the use of an astrologer to further a love affair in Dryden's *An Evening's Love: or, the Mock Astrologer* (1671). Kite's brief, burlesque attempts at astrological jargon reflect the amusement created by Congreve's sincere astrologer Foresight in *Love for Love*. Willard Connely has argued that Kite's harangue at the beginning of the play has an analogue in Volpone's mountebank speech in Jonson's *Volpone*, II.i, but this connection seems tenuous.[8]

Character-patterns like the balance of rake-hero, (relatively) romantic second male lead, and coxcomb, against witty girl, coquette (or serious girl), and clever maid, and also such plot-devices as forged letters, masks, and breeches, are commonplaces of Restoration comedy. James has noticed that Silvia's use of a male disguise resembles in several points those of Leanthe in *Love and a Bottle*, Angelica in *Sir Harry Wildair*, and Oriana in *The Inconstant*, but is distinguished in that 'breeches seem so much more natural to Silvia', and in the more effective operation of the device on the plot level.[9]

---

[7] Preface to *The Twin Rivals* (Stonehill, I, 286); accidentals modernized.

[8] Willard Connely, *Young George Farquhar* (London, 1949), p. 244.

[9] James, pp. 220–2, 228–9.

She has obvious family resemblances to her predecessor-heroines, as Plume has in different ways to Farquhar's earlier heroes – Roebuck in *Love and a Bottle*, Sir Harry Wildair and Colonel Standard in *The Constant Couple* and its sequel, Mirabel and Duretete in *The Inconstant*, and Captain Basil in *The Stage-Coach*. Plume is a gay rake, yet also, like Standard or Duretete, a soldier who is serious about his profession and finally about his love. It would be rash to deny that the author put into each of these characters something of himself (as he would like to be, especially), equally so to see in any one of them a self-portrait. The author was concerned to explore the established figure of the normative Restoration comic hero, 'a Compound of practical Rake and speculative Gentleman', as well as ideas about society, war and the profession of soldiering.[10] Moreover, he knew his actors, and was concerned to write another good part for Wilks, as well as for Anne Oldfield, Estcourt, Cibber, and the rest.[11] Without dismissing the importance of observation of life, I am in general agreement with James's conclusion 'that *The Recruiting Officer* really owes more to Farquhar's experiences in the theatre than it does to his experiences in Shrewsbury . . . [It] grows out of materials, forms, and thoughts that Farquhar worked with all during his career' (p. 257).

THE PLAY

The Recruiting Officer, and its successor *The Beaux' Stratagem*, are acknowledged as the latest masterpieces of Restoration comedy, with a difference indeed, yet still native to the world of Congreve's *Love for Love* or Vanbrugh's *Relapse*. If, after 1700, the Restoration comic spirit had been in retreat, there is nothing decadent in *The Recruiting Officer*, rather, in Leigh Hunt's words, 'a charm of gaiety and good humour throughout . . . We seem to breathe the clear, fresh, ruddy-making air of a remote country town, neighboured by hospitable elegance'.[12]

The play is most original in its combining of the modes of Restoration comedy with a sympathetic and relatively realistic treatment of a country-town society. In the comedies of the time, country people had almost always been measured against the standards of London gentility and caricatured either as boorish clodpates or absurdly inept pretenders to town sophistication. Here 'all

---

[10] Stonehill, I, 51; James, pp. 220, 228–38.

[11] Sybil Rosenfeld, 'Notes on *The Recruiting Officer*', *Theatre Notebook*, XVIII (1963–64), 47–8.

[12] Hunt, p. lxxiv.

the variety and sense of real life that enhanced the traditional London
scene are transferred to Shrewsbury; and Shrewsbury values become
the normative values of the play' (Rothstein, p. 131). Farquhar's
country town Justice is declared to be true to life, 'a worthy, honest,
generous gentleman . . . of as good an understanding as I could give
him', implicitly as an answer to the most elaborate example of the
booby squire stereotype, Sir Wilfull Witwoud of Shropshire in *The
Way of the World*.[13] Justice Balance nonetheless is shown as sometimes fallible, both as a father and a judge. By shifting his milieu,
Farquhar has gained the added advantage of independence from the
contemporary polarizing of stances about human nature between
cynics and sentimentalists, allowing him to express an unusually
genial though clearsighted view of men's frailties.

The author's own enjoyment of his experiences in Shrewsbury
pervades the play. The impression of 'fresh air' Hunt speaks of has
a firm basis in that for more than half its length the action is set out
of doors, in the marketplace or on the walks beside the Severn. In the
part of the play preceding Act IV, scene ii the outdoor-indoor ratio
is five-to-one. Even the indoor scenes are permeated with references
to 'the sharp air from the Welsh mountains', galloping 'after the
hunting-horn', the activity of the poacher, who 'kills all the hares and
partridges within five mile round', or to the wider vista of continental
campaigning.

In presenting the life of Shrewsbury sympathetically Farquhar
was taking further a trend in some earlier relatively minor plays of
the period.[14] He allows, however, for the dominant comic attitude of
scorn for provincial characters by focusing it on his lower-class
characters, the peasants Tummas and Costar, Rose and Bullock,
though even they are made likeable and at times surprisingly shrewd.
Conventional complaints about the noise, dirt, and scandal of the
Town are incongruously advanced by Melinda against Shrewsbury.
Allowed a rich mixture of human types, and of civilized values with
healthy rusticity, Shrewsbury is made an analogue rather than a foil
to the London world, and a microcosm of civilian society. The primary
duality is rather between this world and the alien world of the army
and of the continental war rumbling away offstage, which initiates

[13] See John Loftis, *Comedy and Society from Congreve to Fielding* (Stanford,
1959), pp. 68–76. References by Sir Wilfull and his brother to Shrewsbury
and 'your friends round the Wrekin' (III.i) suggest that Congreve is the
'libel'-writer particularly glanced at in Farquhar's prologue.
[14] e.g. William Cavendish, *The Triumphant Widow* (1667); Thomas Shadwell,
Bury Fair (1689); Thomas Jevon, *The Devil of a Wife* (1686); Thomas
Durfey, *The Bath: or, The Western Lass* (1701) and *The Old Mode & the New,
or Country Miss with her Furbeloe* (1703), set in Coventry.

the action by its intrusion into Shrewsbury to demand its 'complement of men'.

The key motif of the play is the interrelation of loving and fighting. Usually the merest commonplace of Restoration imagery, it has here provided Farquhar with the means of resolving with unusual grace the artistic problem of endowing an entertaining variety of comic material with a satisfying degree of coherence. As the two wooing plot-strands concerning Plume and Silvia, Worthy and Melinda, wear the guise of warfare, so do Plume's recruiting ploys take on to one degree or another the forms of seduction. Structurally, one of the favourite patterns of Restoration comedy, the combination of two love actions with a topic action (cf. Etherege's *The Man of Mode*), has been integrated primarily through the activities of the central figure, Captain Plume, who is at once the rakish lover-hero and the soldier engaged in the occupation of recruiting. Even his love-making takes on 'a businesslike importance as he woos country girls' like Rose or Molly, 'to lure their brothers and sweethearts into the army'. He also takes over the running of Worthy's campaign to win the hand of Melinda. As James observes, 'Plume is perhaps Farquhar's best hero in the sense that he sets plots in motion', and the forms they take derive from his breezy personality (p. 220).

Silvia likewise links two plot-strands and initiates action. When the accident of her brother's death has suddenly made her the next inheritor of her father's estate, the latter adopts a blocking role in relation to her match with Plume, making her promise not to dispose of herself to any man without his consent (II.ii). Plume is too preoccupied with his duties and Worthy's affairs, too realistic about the disproportion in social status that has arisen between them, and too little aware of the real nature of the block, to respond actively to news of her departure into the country. Silvia then assumes a 'pursuing heroine' role and seizes upon the device of disguising herself in breeches as a prospective gentleman-volunteer, 'Jack Wilful'. This not only enables her to engineer a situation in which her father will 'consent' through legally impressing her to serve as a soldier under Plume's command; it also gives her the power to eliminate Rose as a short-term rival in love, and to learn more about her lover before committing herself. In this fashion she successfully recruits Plume into her world through the very means by which he believes he is recruiting 'Jack Wilful' into his. From the time of her entry in disguise in Act III, scene ii, this wooing action is woven into the recruiting action to the extent that the two gain a measure of ironic identity.

Even in the introduction of the well-worn breeches device, an air of naturalness is preserved in the working of the plot. As suggested in the previous section, Silvia's sprightly, enterprising personality and healthy sentiments, and her understanding of the rake she loves, evidenced in Act I, scene ii, make the male disguise seem far more natural to her than to most comic heroines who have used it; and her later appearance as 'Jack Wilful' is prepared for here 'by having Melinda mention four times . . . that Silvia would make a good man'.[15] Indeed the last of these ('You begin to fancy yourself in breeches in good earnest . . .') might be taken to have suggested the scheme.

Other characters too have double functions. Mr Balance as a Justice of the Peace helps Plume in drafting conscripts, but opposes him in his wooing. Brazen, Worthy's rival in love, is Plume's in recruiting.

The second love-action, of the 'difficult girl' type, is comparably bedevilled by the girl's unexpectedly becoming an heiress, a parallel daringly highlighted in Worthy's remark to Plume, 'I can't forbear admiring the equality of our two fortunes' (III.i, 1). The effect, however, is reversed: Melinda's new wealth, and hence social status, removes the external obstacle that in Worthy's eyes had made her ineligible as a wife, but it also gives her the power to create conflict through her resentment of his earlier efforts to make her his kept mistress. Accordingly she snubs him and mildly encourages a rival, until the fear that she may lose him in earnest overcomes her objections. This plot strand is related to the others on several levels. The soldiers, Brazen, Plume, and Kite, each take a part in it. The play's love-war imagery receives its most extended and witty exploration in Worthy's account of how he had besieged, blockaded, and finally tried to take by storm the obdurately chaste Melinda (I.i, 170–96). Brazen and Worthy come to the very edge of a duel for the love of Melinda in Act V, scene v. This in turn parallels the episode in Act III, scene ii when Plume, the serious professional soldier who has refused to fight with Brazen over a woman, Melinda, does fight with him briefly over a recruit – ironically the transvestite Silvia. Once again, a common plot-device, the indecisive duel, is given freshness and thematic value. This strand also reflects the play's other themes, including men's adoption of disguise to further their purposes, and the universality of self-interest.

The dramatic interest in this action derives mainly from the farcical situations that swirl around Melinda, especially in the antics of Brazen, Kite, and her maid Lucy. There is some bite in Kenneth Muir's comment that 'Worthy is dull and acts only as a foil to Plume;

[15] James, p. 221.

Melinda is likewise a foil to Silvia and her actions are determined by the necessities of the plot'.[16] Nonetheless, both characters have a few bright moments, especially, for Melinda, in I.ii and V.iii.

The society within which the two love affairs take place is firmly stratified, indeed more firmly in the world of manners comedy than it was in contemporary life. It was necessary for heroes and heroines to be gentlemen and gentlewomen, and to maintain such a status one must either inherit money or marry it or both. Plume is exceptional among Restoration heroes in that he is actively pursuing a profession. Here Farquhar is fortunate in that the only profession acceptable for a gentleman in the comedy world is that of military officer, and the only soldier who can be active rather than 'resting' within the normal social environment is the officer assigned to recruiting. Even so, Plume's income as captain makes him suitable 'for a bare son-in-law' but not for the heir by marriage to Balance's 'estate and family' (II.ii, 20–1).

> Wealth is only slightly less important than love as a motivating force in [Restoration] comedies, and the amount of wealth, which is often in the form of a landed estate, is described as precisely as is the condition of the heroine's affections . . . Silvia has £1,500 before her brother dies, whereupon she becomes heiress to £1,200 a year.[17]

Worthy's attitude to Melinda is typical of the unsentimental view of comic heroes like Aimwell in *The Beaux' Stratagem* that 'no woman can be a beauty without a fortune'. While she lacked it, he tried to make her his mistress with a settlement of £500 a year, but with £20,000 of her own she is a match to be sought after. Her 'difficultness' appears at first to stem from the coquette's delight in power, but later we perceive its basis in the natural response of a self-respecting and touchy woman to his past treatment –

> Remember the wicked insinuations, artful baits, deceitful arguments, cunning pretences; then your impudent behaviour, loose expressions, familiar letters, rude visits; remember those, those, Mr Worthy.   (V.iii, 30–3)

These are balanced against his claim that she is in his debt: 'my fears, sighs, vows, promises, assiduities, anxieties, jealousies, have run on for a whole year, without any payment' (V.iii, 24–6). On Melinda's suggestion they decide to balance one 'account' against the other, 'come to an agreement', and 'begin upon a new score'. Evidently they love one another, but communicate successfully only when both abandon romantic sentiment. Plume may well be unique

[16] *The Comedy of Manners* (London, 1970), p. 149.
[17] Loftis, op. cit., pp. 42–8.

among Restoration heroes in professing to like Silvia less after she has come into a substantial fortune; still, it makes possible a more completely happy-ever-after resolution, in enabling him to give up his risky profession.

The recruiting action has been aptly described as 'almost a comic documentary' upon the working of the Impressment Acts (Rothstein, p. 129). In the background of the play, as the enemy of comedy, is the War of the Spanish Succession, extending from 1702 to 1713 but in reality the struggle that had begun in 1688 between the France of Louis XIV and the main Grand Alliance powers, England, the Netherlands, and the Austro-German Empire. England had begun this struggle with a relatively negligible field-army, and even in 1702 had a mere 18,000 men under arms. In 1708–09 it had about 70,000, and was playing a major part in Marlborough's continental battles. The activities of its Plumes and Kites, sent off recruiting while it was in winter quarters, were essential to the war effort.[18]

The first type of recruiting instituted in this era was beating up for volunteers, who would receive 40s. enlistment money. In the play Kite's straightforward appeal for volunteers has no success at all, but creates an opportunity to get two of the local lads drunk and trick them into taking 'the Queen's money'. We see him bamboozling two more, the smith and the butcher, with his fortune-telling routine. In the case of the butcher, Kite presumably hopes his mother will part with her hundred pounds to buy his discharge.

By 1703 it had become clear that voluntary enlistment would not in itself raise enough men, and the first of several Impressment Acts were introduced, 2° and 3° Annae Reginæ, chapters XIII and XIX. The latter empowered three Justices of the Peace to 'raise and levy such Able-bodied Men as have not any lawful calling or Employment, or visible Means for their Maintenance and Livelihood, to serve as Soldiers'. This left to the Justices concerned great liberty in interpretation, and some High Tory Justices were unco-operative, but moderate Tory or Whig Justices, like those in Shropshire in real life and in the play, could be very helpful, even to the extent of bending the law.[19] The recruit so conscripted was to receive 20s. levy-money, and the constable or parish officer responsible for raising him, up to 10s.; hence the 11s. bribe for which the constable lets men run away (V.v, 167–9). A third class of conscripts is noticed but not given prominence: the convicted criminals, the sheep-stealers and the horse-thief (V.iv, 4–6), who are enlisted rather than hanged.

A brief survey of the design of the play and the development of its

[18] George Macaulay Trevelyan, *England under Queen Anne: Blenheim* (London, 1930), pp. 216–21.
[19] ibid. pp. 218–19.

themes will provide further evidence of skilful craftsmanship. A light-heartedly equivocal attitude to recruiting, and the military world it serves, emerges in the epigraph and prologue, which mock-heroically invest them with the dimensions of the Trojan War. The 'arts' by which Ulysses entices Achilles to go off to fight play an essential role in ensuring the Greek victory, yet the baits offered here, instead of undying fame, are 'plunder, fine laced coats and glitt'ring arms'. The allusion to the Wooden Horse in the epigraph likewise emphasizes the slyness of the means by which even the most glorious wars are won.[20]

Act I begins with the bustling intrusion of Sergeant Kite and his drummer into the peaceful marketplace to incite men to glory and greatness. That the 'freedom' he offers from everyday bondages is simply a more extreme form of servitude will be demonstrated in Act II, scene iii, once he has Appletree and Pearmain under orders. The claim that enlistment will transform lower-class people into gentlemen will be belied by Kite's own 'character' of himself in Act III, scene i, as a proletarian in a class-conscious army, who will never rise higher than sergeant. In introducing the motif of soldier-ing as an alternative to marriage, he is wholly truthful only in his black jokes about 'the bed of honour'. Through the arrival of Plume and then Worthy, the exposition is provided for the two love-actions; and Plume learns to his surprise that the bastard he has had by a local girl is being treated kindly by Silvia, for love of him. Schneider comments that the 'supreme act of generosity belongs to Silvia . . . who shows what a *woman* of honour is made of'.[21]

The second scene allows the two heroines to show their mettle, in raillery that turns from playfulness to civil insults. Silvia attacks her cousin's newly acquired social 'airs' and her harsh treatment of Worthy. She shows herself eager to secure Plume, and unconcerned about his philandering:

> Constancy is but a dull, sleepy quality at best, they will hardly admit it among the manly virtues; nor do I think it deserves a place with bravery, knowledge, policy, justice, and some other qualities that are proper to that noble sex.   (I.ii, 49–52)

The meaning of a statement like this by Silvia or Plume is ironically modified by its dramatic context, and especially by its function in the social gamesmanship of the moment. Silvia speaks like a gay female rake, yet her appeal to natural robust sanity approaches the stance of a woman of sense, and she intends that her own constancy

[20] cf. epigraph footnote.
[21] Ben Ross Schneider Jr, *The Ethos of Restoration Comedy* (Urbana, Illinois, 1971), p. 64.

will supply the deficiency in her lover. She will demonstrate that she shares with Plume the comic virtues of 'bravery, knowledge, policy, justice', also a taste for the plain and unhypocritical, including sexual frankness, and a respect for high spirits. She surpasses him in her ability to maintain a poise between natural and civilized values.

In the first scene of Act II Balance is welcoming Plume both as a soldier and a suitor to his daughter; and Plume's interview with the lady herself is full of gallantry, but is cut short before it can reach any kind of resolution. Balance has received news of his son's impending death, and his reaction in scene ii is to try and put Silvia beyond Plume's reach, to preserve her for a match more worthy of her new status. Melinda's attempt at mischief-making by letter is defused by Worthy. The third scene is devoted to the recruitment of two country lads through Kite's tricks and Plume's cajolery, that lead to their cheerfully accepting enlistment.

Act III, scene i provides complication through the introduction of new characters, Rose and her brother, and Brazen. Plume's decision not to pursue Silvia into the country frees him to try to seduce Rose, in order to recruit her brother and admirers. The self-display of Brazen advances the Melinda-Worthy action, for in the following scene he pursues his tiresome courtship of Melinda. It is in scene ii on the Severn walks that Silvia first appears in male disguise, thus partially uniting two of the plots, and both Plume and Brazen endeavour to recruit her. Act IV, scene i carries straight on, with closer intimacy developing between Plume and his prize 'recruit'. These three scenes contain a number of sequences advancing each of the plot-strands, articulated fairly elegantly by *liaison des scènes*. The third of them contains Plume's striking revelation of his moral stance to the disguised Silvia. His seduction of Rose, though thwarted by his landlady, has fulfilled its purpose in drawing in recruits and he will not take a 'common woman' to bed in her place.

> No, faith, I'm not that rake that the world imagines; I have got an air of freedom which people mistake for lewdness in me, as they mistake formality in others for religion; the world is all a cheat, only I take mine which is undesigned to be more excusable than theirs, which is hypocritical; I hurt nobody but myself, and they abuse all mankind. – Will you lie with me? (IV.i, 167–73)

This speech has been criticized for introducing an element of sentimentalism as a 'sudden sop to the prudes', for inconsistency, and for technical crudeness. Within the plot it enables us to accept that Plume, like Balance, will make a good husband once he is settled down in domestic life. It obviates the need for a fifth-act conversion from hard-line libertine values to conventional Christian moralism.[22] Rather, the ethics of the play appear to be those of Locke, inductive, empirical, and in part special to each society, present implicitly, in the consciousness of the dramatist but beyond the capability of the characters to deal with in abstract terms. Rothstein has argued that 'Plume's self-defence is thematically necessary' in that it contributes to a demonstration that the army does not, after all,

> corrupt . . . the civil proprieties [to an extent that would] under-mine the strength of social order that the whole play justifies, and that makes the whole play work. If Farquhar seems to indict the army along with Plume at the beginning, in deference to the popular notion of scandal and danger, he quickly turns to a rhetoric that reverses original expectations and reclaims the honour of his army.
>
> (p. 138)

The wider issue here is controversial. It has been cogently argued by Eugene James that Farquhar's play, far from being 'pro-war' and 'characterized by . . . dry-eyed patriotic militarism' as Rothstein believes (p. 132), demonstrates in a thoroughgoing fashion the 'immorality and cruelty' of the military world, and its author's 'hatred of war' (James, pp. 236, 241). However, the civilian world is little better, though its members

> hide their sins under a mantle of goodness . . . The soldier, thus, appears as worse than he is, while the civilian appears better than he is, but they are the same weak, sinful human beings beneath their poses, and somehow the soldier's pose is more honest (and this is the great virtue of Plume) than the civilian's. At least it is simpler and easier to read in the soldier's pose the truth about mankind.
>
> (James, p. 252)

It may be noticed, further, that 'hypocritical' in Restoration comic tradition generally alludes to the puritans, and especially the puri-tanically inclined merchant-class. This class was supposedly prov-iding the main support for the Society for the Reformation of Manners, which was waging war against the theatres and the relatively harmless sexual freedoms of their comic heroes. At the same time certain of its members were subverting both the military order and the civilian order in their quest for profits at the national expense.

Act IV, scene ii is the longest in the play, and is dominated by Kite, in the guise of Copernicus the fortune-teller. It advances both the recruiting action and the Melinda-Worthy action. He excites the greed and vanity of a blacksmith and a butcher, so as to persuade them to volunteer. Then Melinda arrives to be told she must come

[22] See David S. Berkeley, 'The Penitent Rake in Restoration Comedy', *Modern Philology*, XLIX (1951–52), 223–33.

to terms with Worthy by the following morning, or lose him forever. Her signature from her letter to Balance is produced in a farcical way that serves to convince her of Copernicus's power. Brazen arrives, and the letter ostensibly from Melinda that he leaves with Kite reveals by its handwriting that his correspondent is really Lucy.

Act V contains seven scenes, beginning early the next morning. The first two portray the arrest of Silvia and Rose, after the latter's frustrating night, and their appearance before Justice Balance. In scene iii Melinda's and Worthy's agreement to betrothal apparently ends this plot-strand; but in scene iv Worthy and Plume are led to believe that Melinda is indeed proposing to elope with Brazen, which generates a little extra excitement.

The court scene that follows is concerned with the impressment of recruits, including the impressment of the disguised Silvia. The Justices' names are Balance, Scale, and Scruple, yet the proceedings are ludicrously improper. Their invitation to Plume to sit with them on the bench provides a visual image of how little impartial they are in judging between the army and the men it wants. Scruple's protests on behalf of the married man and the miner are quite ineffectual. Still, the discovery that the former is a poacher with a daftly prolific wife, and that the second has tried to cheat the system with bribes and lies, prevents them retaining too much of our sympathy. The most amusing episode of the play follows, as Silvia, alias 'Jack Wilful' alias 'Pinch', insults them and mocks her own father. All three Justices hasten to order her impressment with no concern for the legality of what they are doing, or for her warnings:

> Once more, gentlemen, have a care what you do, for you shall severely smart for any violence you offer to me; and you, Mr Balance, I speak to you particularly, you shall heartily repent it.
>
> (V.v, 136–9)

A chilling note is provided in the reading of the Articles of War,[23] but the scene ends humorously with the constable of the court being himself threatened with impressment in place of the men he has allowed to run away.

In scene vi Worthy arrives in time to frustrate Lucy's attempt to bring about a masked marriage with Brazen.

The final scene brings together all the main characters, but is quieter in tone than the court scene. Its only action concerns the recognition by Balance of how his daughter has tricked him. His dignity is preserved when he secures her discharge from Plume and then voluntarily consents to their marriage. Plume responds with a succession of gallant antitheses, but does not try too hard to disguise

[23] See Appendix 4.

his joy and relief in leaving his dangerous and precarious profession. He has after all ostensibly done his share of fighting shortly before, at the Battle of Blenheim. The minor third parties in the two love triangles are disposed of neatly. Rose is assigned to Silvia's care, and Brazen is to be given Plume's recruits. He will march them off to fight perhaps, at Ramillies in May 1706, or to join Farquhar's own unit which, under new command as Sir Thomas Prendergast's Regiment of Foot, would cross to Flanders in 1708 and take part the following year in 'the very murdering battle' of Malplaquet.[24]

Here and there Farquhar has planted indictments of the army system and its officers for their vicious inefficiency and corruption. And the obligatory reading of the Articles of War against mutiny and desertion, in which every conceivable offence is punishable by death, cannot but produce a dark shadow in the hitherto amusing court-room scene. Warfare itself is seen as grim rather than glorious. Even so, in the immediate past is set Marlborough's famous victory at Blenheim, England's first great victory on land since Agincourt. Plume is entitled to exploit its warm afterglow; and to mouth a few platitudes about glory yielding full return for life, once he can afford to resign his commission.

Arthur Bedford in *The Evil and Danger of Stage Plays* (Bristol, 1706) ferociously assailed *The Recruiting Officer* as destructive of patriotism and slanderous about the average character of the nation's military officers. He wildly overstates his case, and shows no sensitivity to the genial tone of the play, so that he takes as deliberate defamation much that is simply humorous realism. Some of the satirical touches he notices are unquestionably intended, as are also some of those cited by James (pp. 240–51). They are, however, given relatively little dramatic emphasis, beside that given to humorous situation, and are balanced against expressions of cheerfully affirmed patriotism ('Huzza for the Queen!'). The effect of each satiric attack upon the army world is modified ironically by its immediate context, and by the pervading atmosphere of good humour. Farquhar's view of human nature was orthodox for his time. 'It was a dual entity; its baser passions were constantly at war with its nobler, and too frequently victorious. In this world, moral perfection was quite unattainable'.[25] Nonetheless, Silvia provides a positive example of what can be achieved in this world through bravery and generous love, and the comic dramatist may ameliorate the condition of man in society by corrective satire.

[24] Charles Dalton, *English Army Lists and Commission Registers, 1661–1714*, 6 vols. (London, 1892–1904, reprint 1960), V, 263–4; VI, 357–8.
[25] Ernest Bernbaum, *The Drama of Sensibility* (1915, rpt. Gloucester, Mass. 1958), p. 3.

Three inconsistencies that have been cited as evidence that the play was casually 'put together' and probably 'never thoroughly reviewed by the author' deserve some attention.[26] One of these, the confusion in the use of '1 Mob' and '2 Mob' as speech prefixes for Tummas and Costar, is discussed in the 'Note on the Text'. An 'error' to which Hough has drawn attention is not necessarily an error at all. Plume knows Silvia in disguise only as 'Jack Wilful', yet makes no demur when in the court scene Balance refers to her as 'Pinch' (V.v, 116); similarly in Act V, scene vii Balance, who has known her only as 'Pinch', tells the servant to 'go to the Captain's lodgings and inquire for Mr Wilful'. In the first case Plume has agreed to go along with any device that 'Jack Wilful' wishes to use to get himself 'impressed by the Act of Parliament' (IV.i, 161–2). In the second, it should be remembered that in Act V, scene vii Balance and Plume have just finished dining together, and may be presumed to have exchanged information about their startlingly impudent young conscript. Plume has had no reason given him for concealing the identity of 'Jack Wilful' from Balance, particularly now the impressment is complete.

Another apparent flaw in the plot-machinery concerns Lucy's third letter to Brazen. In Act V, scene iv what convinces Plume, and hence Worthy, that Melinda is indeed going off with Brazen, and so makes scene vi possible, is that the latter shows Plume the bottom only of this letter, and he recognizes that it bears Melinda's genuine signature. Lucy has induced Melinda to sign her name on a blank sheet of paper in Act IV, scene ii and then used it to write this letter in order to further her campaign to trick Brazen into marriage with herself. The difficulty that arises is that in Act IV, scene ii Brazen had left in Kite's hands the second of two love letters to himself, purportedly from Melinda, and Worthy recognized as soon as he saw it that it was 'Lucy's hand', which he states is 'no more like Melinda's character than black is to white' (IV.ii, 335–6). His belief that Melinda is in no way implicated with Brazen is crucial to his reconciliation with her in Act V, scene iii. Now it seems absurd that when Lucy has written twice to Brazen using her own handwriting, she should in her third letter want to use Melinda's signature and risk having him recognize that it is unlike her earlier forgeries. We were not told on the previous occasion whether the signature was like Melinda's own and are left to presume it was not, since the letter was compared with Melinda's genuine signature from her own letter to Balance. One is obliged to accept that there is an

[26] Robert L. Hough, 'An Error in *The Recruiting Officer*', *N & Q*, CXCVIII (1953), 340–1; and 'Farquhar: *The Recruiting Officer*', *N & Q*, CXCIX (1954), 474; Rothstein, p. 131.

inconsistency here, but it seems a fault of intractable over-ingenuity rather than casualness.

Two characters deserve further mention. Kite is the play's most original and amusing figure, and provides its best character role. He tends to dominate any episode he is involved in through his eloquence, sardonic humour, resourcefulness, and 'rare ingenious knavery', such as had delighted the Elizabethans.[27] His set-piece character of himself in Act III, scene i suggests an intriguing degree of self-awareness.

Brazen provides a foil to Plume as recruiting officer and to both Plume and Worthy as lovers, as of brass to gold. Chatterer though he is, and hopelessly lazy in pursuing his trade, he does not lack a kind of wit. Nor, vitally, does he lack courage, but fights Plume briefly, and trumps Worthy's belligerence with the perfectly terrifying proposal to fight a pistol duel with both men standing on a cloak. He escapes punishment for his folly, in avoiding marriage to Lucy, and is rewarded for his incompetence with the gain of Plume's recruits. Rothstein relates this escape to the wider issue of a development of a drama emphasizing relationships between characters, in Farquhar's last two plays, replacing the drama that emphasized individual characters, to be duly rewarded or punished (pp. 167–70).

Farquhar's dialogue has been described by Pope as 'low' and 'pert', by Oldmixon as 'loose and incorrect' yet 'gay and agreeable'.[28] In many cases 'lowness' and, grammatically, 'looseness' and 'incorrectness', are entirely proper to the speaker, and Farquhar must be regarded as one of the pioneers in the development of lifelike, naturalistic stage speech. He has discovered that the juxtapositional modes of normal speech differ from those of formal grammar, and developed a means of presenting them, particularly effective in the mouths of Kite and Brazen. The peasant characters, Pearmain, Appletree, Rose, and Bullock, are given a slight but adequately distinguishing dialect and turn of phrase, that have nothing to do with stage-bumpkinery.

The speech modes given to the gentlemen and ladies preserve, usually in relaxed, unobtrusive form, the patterns of Restoration wit: antithesis, paradox, simile. In Act III, scene ii, when Plume declares he is drunk enough to fancy himself 'mighty witty', he produces at once a semi-personifying antithesis ('Reason still keeps its throne, but it nods a little') and a dreadful punning simile ('As fit [for a frolic] as close pinners for a punk in the pit'), extends

---

[27] Jonson, *Volpone*, V.i, 14; cf. John V. Curry, *Deception in Elizabethan Comedy* (Chicago, 1955).

[28] Pope, 'Imitation of "The First Epistle of the Second Book of Horace"', (1737); [John Oldmixon], *The Muses Mercury* (May 1707), cited in James, p. 17.

Worthy's metaphor of Melinda as ship, then goes on to out-banter Brazen.

There is relatively little dialogue that is not dramatically active: even Brazen and Plume's topical chat in V.iv about the theatre and privateer as rival investments serves to lead up to the disclosure of Brazen's expectation of marrying Melinda. There is little general reflection and only two 'characters' to briefly halt the action. 'The comedy . . . rests on its characters . . . and its intrigues . . . Although there are flashes of wit . . . the characters are too busy intriguing to carry on much witty talk and are really outside the pale of high society' (James, p. 303).

The tone even of Plume's or Silvia's speeches is in Pope's sense 'pert', yet the limitations in their sensibilities are fitting to their situations, and their voices, like those of every other character from highest to lowest, are human and alive.[29] The presiding sensibility is the author's: it does not receive direct expression through the mouth of any one character; instead, meaning is created through characters in interaction.

William Archer in his preface to the first Mermaid edition of Farquhar's plays rightly drew attention to the degree to which, in his sense, Farquhar was a pure dramatist, and not, as many of his Restoration predecessors were, a mixture of dramatist and essayist. In *The Recruiting Officer* Farquhar has created a masterpiece of theatre in which human resourcefulness triumphs over chance and social restriction, and good-natured satire is mixed with humour. Critical discussion of comedies of this era has taken rather far the retrospective creation of genre pigeon-holes, and valued over-exclusively the comedy of wit. In talking about this play some comparisons with other comedies of the time are needful, yet it deserves to be experienced and enjoyed for itself as 'a comedy of life'.[30]

STAGE HISTORY

The initial production at the Drury Lane theatre scored an immediate success, achieving a first run of eight performances, on 8, 9, 10, 12, 13, 15, 17, and 20 April. The curiously broken nature of this run helps to explain the strategy of Farquhar's epilogue, and also the care he took to provide his play with songs and music. It was interrupted by the performances on 11 April of Bononcini's opera

[29] Exception might be made of some speeches in Act V, scene vii, which tend to conventional public rhetoric.
[30] Strauss, p. liii.

Camilla, on 16 April of Rochester's tragedy *Valentinian*, and on 18 April of Motteux's semi-opera *The Island Princess*. The theatre audience had developed a passion for music it was shrewd to cater to.

In the original cast, for whom the play was designed, it is evident that Richard Estcourt particularly distinguished himself as Kite. Steele rather grudgingly commented upon a later performance in *The Tatler* of 25 May 1709 that Estcourt's 'proper Sense and Observation is what supports the Play. There is not, in my humble Opinion, the Humour hit in *Sergeant Kite*, but it is admirably supply'd by his Action'.

The play had already proved able to support itself without Estcourt: most of the original cast had joined Owen Swiney at the Queen's Theatre, Haymarket, and presented the play, with Pack as Kite, on 14, 18, and 30 November. The rebuilt Drury Lane troupe presented it on 24 October, on 1 November, and in direct competition on 30 November, offering the drawcard of 'The true Serjeant Kite'. Certainly this is a marvellous role for a humorous character-actor, but Estcourt, a gifted mimic, excelled in it: 'every night of performance [he] entertained the audience with a variety of little catches and flights of humour, that pleased all but his critics'.[31]

As Sybil Rosenfeld has shown, the contrasted characterization of the other central characters is 'excellently fitted' to 'the contrast in acting temperaments' of Wilks as Plume, Cibber as Brazen, Anne Oldfield as Silvia, and Jane Rogers as Melinda. Steele made the general comment that '*Wilks* has a singular Talent in representing the Graces of Nature, *Cibber* the Deformity in the Affectation of them'.[32] Wilks was gentlemanly, 'graceful, gay, sprightly, and quite without affectation', Cibber, a gifted presenter of fops and cox-combs: 'a good deal of the fun . . . must have been in witnessing these two fine comedians demonstrate the difference between gold and pinchbeck' (Rosenfeld, p. 48).

Anne Oldfield 'was the perfect, gay woman of quality as a match for Plume; tall, very beautiful, with a fine figure and a remarkable silver voice . . . Mrs Rogers, on the other hand, was of a darker character . . . [she] had a reputation for prudery and would play none but the virtuous'.

In the lesser parts Farquhar has evidently exploited the lucky chances of having a large comic actor, William Bullock, for his country boy 'Bullock', and a 'tiny little man with a squealing voice', Henry Norris, for the courageous Costar Pearmain (ibid).

Performances since the first run have been extremely numerous.

[31] William Rufus Chetwood, cited in Sybil Rosenfeld, 'Notes on *The Recruiting Officer*', op. cit.
[32] *Tatler*, No. 182, 6–8 June 1710.

Arthur Bedford records that during the summer off-season in 1706 the play was presented at Bristol on 24 and 25 July, and Genest, that it appeared in Bath on 16 September.[33] Its regular appearance as a stock play, particularly in the first weeks of each theatrical season, is amply documented in the volumes of *The London Stage, 1660–1800*. Michael Shugrue has noticed that between 1706 and 1776 it appeared 447 times without missing a single season (p. xx); while between 1776 and 1800 it appeared on another 49 occasions, missing only five seasons.[34] Stonehill (II, 39) states that 'throughout the nineteenth century [it] was one of the most popular plays in the repertory of provincial companies'.

The most noteworthy productions in this century have been those at the Arts Theatre, London, in November 1943–January 1944, with Trevor Howard as Plume, and at the Old Vic, opening on 10 December 1963, as the fourth production of the National Theatre Company. This latter, directed by William Gaskill, is admirably documented in Kenneth Tynan's *'The Recruiting Officer'*: *The National Theatre Production*, published in 1965. Some side-notes from this book appear in footnotes in the present edition. Gaskill's production gave full value to the pursuit of the game of love as if it were a military campaign, compared to the seductive gamesmanship of recruiting. It went much further though in extending the darkly satiric, anti-heroic possibilities of the text, following the lead of Bertolt Brecht's imitation of Farquhar's play, *Pauken und Trompetten* (1955), which is set in the context of the American War of Independence.[35] The relatively greater emphasis upon the recruiting aspect over the romantic aspect of the play is stressed by Gaskill's handling of the ending: after the economically advantageous marriage-promises,

> Kite leads on his ragged band of recruits, with the collier's wife, a solitary camp-follower, bringing up the rear. Plume hands them over to Brazen, who leads them off.   (Tynan, p. 138)

More in keeping with Farquhar's spirit, one feels, was an incident about the middle of the eighteenth century, when James Quin, playing Justice Balance, was decidedly drunk, and in Act II, scene ii, demanded of Peg Woffington, 'Silvia, what age were you when your dear mother married?' She remained silent, so he tried again: 'I ask what age you were when your mother was born'.[36]

---

[33] Bedford, op. cit., p. 150; Genest, see Appendix 2.

[34] *The London Stage*, Part V, *passim*.

[35] See Albert Wertheim, 'Bertolt Brecht and George Farquhar's *The Recruiting Officer*', *Comparative Drama*, VII (1973), 179–80.

[36] *Anecdotes of the Theatre*, ed. A. H. Engelbach (London, 1914), p. 183 (slightly different from the version in Stonehill, II, 38).

NOTE ON THE TEXT

THE FIRST QUARTO was issued on, or just before, 3 May 1706, when the play was advertised in the *Daily Courant* as 'Newly published . . .', with the three asterisks then customary to signal first publication.[1] Recent editors have thought this quarto (hereafter Q1) came out on 12 April, four days after the first performance; but the evidence cited, a statement appended to a *Daily Courant* advertisement for the fourth performance, that 'This Play is Sold by' Knapton and Lintott, was clearly a declaration of intent only, and appeared in this newspaper in a slightly different form ('These Plays are Sold by . . .') on 6, 8, and 9 April. Publication of the second edition, 'corrected', was announced in the same paper on 23 May, and of the third on 6 December.[2] Though the latter came out before Farquhar's death, in May 1707, its variants are minor and can safely be attributed to the printing-house. Lacking any authority, it will in general be ignored. The play has since been reprinted many times, separately or in various collections, some of the most interesting texts being those that represent acting-versions, discussed in Appendix 1.

The description of the second quarto (Q2) as 'corrected' is just, as its text contains extensive and systematic alterations, ranging from minor variations in spelling or punctuation to deletion of one short scene, and substitution of new versions of two passages of dialogue.[3] The main issue of editorial debate concerns the degree of secondary authority to be accorded to the numerous substantive variations in Q2. Was Farquhar responsible for each of them, and if so, was he revising, to improve the theatrical or literary effectiveness of his text, or was he acting under duress, to make it more acceptable to the Master of the Revels (the censor of stage-scripts) and to others who objected to profane or indecent dialogue?

The manuscript that served as copy-text for Q1 is separated from Q2 by several stages of modification. The Q1 compositors would have supplied some standardization of accidentals, probably also of diction, and introduced minor misprints. The parallel manuscript that went to the theatre would have been altered to improve its theatrical effectiveness, before and maybe after the first night. Farquhar, as a friend of Wilks and Anne Oldfield, his Plume and Silvia, and a constant frequenter of the Drury Lane theatre while in

[1] Also in the *Post-man*, 2–4 May 1706.
[2] The *Daily Courant*, 28 November 1706, promised publication of the third edition on 3 December.
[3] A near-complete list of variants in Q1–3 is provided in Jeffares, pp. 111–40.

London and in adequate health, would have been on hand to do any rewriting needed. The Master of the Revels may have required some cuts before licensing the play for performance. Farquhar himself, as seems evident from the very detailed nature of some of the variants, then prepared the copy-text for Q2 by marking up a copy of Q1. Finally, the Q2 compositor(s) imposed very extensive standardization of accidentals, expansion of elided word-forms, and substitution of phrases that were more elevated or grammatically correct, often gravely reducing the colloquial vigour, vividness, and rhythmic qualities of the original dialogue.

Bernard Lintott's accounts record that on 12 February 1706 he paid Farquhar £16 2s.6d. for the publication rights, and presumably he received at that time the manuscript that would serve as copy-text for Q1.[4] While Q2 was evidently set from a marked-up copy of Q1 after the script had stood the test of performance, the Q1 text had probably not even received the benefit of testing in rehearsals, to correct minor flaws and confusions. This seems indicated by the vagueness in the use of the speech-prefixes 'Mob' in Act I, scene i, and '1st Mob' and '2d Mob' in Act II, scene iii (this does not receive correction in Q2). In the latter scene the character eventually named as Costar Pearmain is denoted by '2d Mob' before Plume's entry, '1st Mob' thereafter, while Thomas Appletree is initially '1st Mob', then '2d Mob'. And it is far from clear that Farquhar intended either man to be the same person as the speaker denoted in Act I, scene i as 'Mob' (i.e., one of the mob), although later eighteenth-century texts presumably followed current theatre-practice in identifying him as Costar Pearmain (there is a minor difficulty, due perhaps to a mere authorial oversight: he can't read, Costar can). The present edition retains the speech prefix 'Mob' in Act I, scene i, though in the later scene it accepts the Q1 'dramatis personae' list designations, Costar Pearmain and Thomas Appletree.[5] Another tangle in Q1 which is resolved in Q2 occurs near the end of Act III, scene i: Rose excuses herself and leaves, Balance makes a remark to himself, then Plume comes in singing and meets with Rose, apparently, on stage. The original intention 'evidently was that Plume should meet Rose outside and bring her back with him. It was doubtless found more effective that Rose should not leave the stage, but that Plume should enter and embrace her, not at first observing

---

Balance'.[6] Q1 juxtaposes both Farquhar's earlier and his revised intentions; Q2, by omitting Rose's and Balance's speeches, lucidly presents the later arrangement.

In other respects Q1 presents a clean, rather carefully set text, consistent enough in its characteristics to be probably mainly the work of a single compositor. In the last sheet, K, the type-size is reduced, to enable the dialogue of the final three scenes to be crowded on to this sheet. Some stage directions were evidently crowded out, including that for the location of Act V, scene vi. The speech-prefix form 'Silv.' rather than 'Sil.' on K2–K2^v, and use of a comma rather than a full stop after full-word prefixes ('Plume', etc.) from K2^v onward, suggests the intervention of another compositor of un-settled habits in the setting of this sheet. The fairly regular recur-rence of certain identifiable running-titles through successive sheets suggests steady presswork.[7] Collation of different copies has revealed no press corrections of textual significance.[8]

Certain kinds of modification observable in the Q2 text can be traced to the printing-house compositor(s): minor misprints, normalization of spelling and punctuation, and substitution of more formal or common alternatives for Farquhar's vigorous, colloquial dialect, word-forms, and phrases. Abbreviated forms are expanded: 'I'm' to 'I am', 'o'th'' to 'of the', 'you're' to 'you are', 'look'e' or 'thank'e' to 'look you', 'thank you'. Dialect forms like 'I'se' or 'Wauns' become 'I'll' or 'Wounds'. The two latter categories of Q2 variants can be confidently rejected.

In some instances, the Q2 reading is more colloquial than Q1's, and the change is presumably Farquhar's, either recording a revision, or restoring an original intention lost in the printing of Q1: 'them', 'that is', 'I will', 'do not', become ''em', 'that's', 'I'll' and 'don't'. In half a dozen cases the cutting of a semi-superfluous 'that' within a phrase tightens up speech-rhythm. Other variants are harder to evaluate.

Farquhar writes with great sensitivity for the ear, not the reader's

---

[6] Archer, p. 292. Michael Shugrue's explanation of the Q2 omission here in terms of deleting an unfavourable reflection on recruiting officers ignores these factors, and the retention of near identical remarks elsewhere, e.g., I.i, 218–20 (Shugrue, p. xi). Cf. G. W. Whiting, 'The Date of the Second Edition of *The Constant Couple'*, *Modern Language Notes*, XLVII (1932), 147–8.

[7] e.g., a title with two nicks in the capital 'O' is identifiable on B4, C4, D4, E4, F4, G3, I2, and K3.

[8] British Museum, 11773.g.11; Victoria and Albert Museum, F4° 6976/22 and F.D. 11.14. Jeffares has collated, in addition, the Bodleian, Scottish National Library, Harvard, and Yale copies (Jeffares, p. 17).

eye, seeking to re-create the manner of natural speech, and to make of it effective stage-dialogue. The result often lacks grammatical precision, and many minor verbal variants in Q2 that supply it are grossly destructive of rhythm, authenticity, and vigour. It cannot, however, be assumed that not one of the changes that improve the grammar, or that give more elevation and polish to the diction, has been introduced by the revising author, conscious that the Q2 text is aimed at the reader, and every such variant must be judged on its merits. In the present edition variants of these kinds which represent positive gain without apparent loss have been adopted, though where the balance of advantage seems indifferent, the Q1 reading has been given the benefit of the doubt, as more probably authorial.

In punctuation, the system of dashes, commas, and semi-colons present in Q1 conveys a fluid, springy, jerky yet coherent speech-manner, very appropriate to certain characters and contexts, e.g., Brazen often talks in a kind of associative gabble. The relatively frequent, short pauses imposed have the effect that no one pause within a speech assumes too much weight. Most punctuation variants in Q2 substitute grammatical for rhetorical pointing, or simplify Q1's combinations of comma-dash or full stop-dash; but in some cases a comma or semi-colon in Q1 is replaced by a dash, perhaps restoring Farquhar's original intention, or finding a more satisfactory means of conveying it. For the present edition, the punctuation of Q1 has usually been retained, as the more valid, but sometimes where this can be done without loss the formally more correct Q2 variant has been adopted. Some commas have been deleted in places where one would naturally supply a pause.

Some stage directions in Q2 are simplified, shortened, and standardized, e.g., 'SCENE *changes to another Apartment*' at the beginning of Act II, scene ii, becomes 'SCENE, *Another Apartment*'; and in Act II, scene iii, '*While they talk, the Captain and Serjeant whisper*' is shortened to '*Captain and Serjeant whisper the while*'. These revisions may be Farquhar's, or at least made with his approval, since they relate to staging. Some directions in Q1 seem addressed to the actor rather than the reader, e.g., in Act V, scene v, 'Kite *and* Constable *advance to the Front of the Stage*', which is altered to 'Kite *and* Constable *advance forward*'. In a few instances, Q1 variants have been retained in the present edition, as they provide clearer information.

While the minor variants so far discussed often make the tone less rough, they do nothing to remove profanities or indecencies. This issue arises in relation to the deletion or rewriting of longer passages.

The theatres were indeed under pressure from the Lord Chamberlain, who several times commanded the Drury Lane company to be sure 'to leve out such Expressions as are contrary to Religion & Good Manners' in plays it performed; while Charles Killigrew, the Master of the Revels, was reported to 'strike out whole Scenes of a vicious, or immoral Character' from new plays.[9] Yet the actors were also under pressure to give their audiences whatever would attract them, in the face of competition from operas, ballad-farces, the rival theatre's plays, and the card-table. Even the citizens had disliked the high moral tone of Farquhar's previous full-length play. And the central contention of Arthur Bedford's *The Evil and Danger of Stage Plays*, published late in 1706, was that despite all the efforts of the reformers the new plays of the past three years were as bad as ever.

It is evident that nearly all the more substantial alterations in Q2 have far more to do with theatrical effectiveness than they do with propriety. The revision in Act IV, scene i is a good example: here, ten lines in French are replaced by some twenty lines in English. Though the French is simple, one may be sure it would not have been understood by most of the footmen in the upper gallery, an important segment of the audience. The obvious feature of Silvia's '*Avez vous couché avec elle?*' is that it is superfluous, for she presents essentially the same question forty lines later ('I must be certified that this girl is a virgin'). Neither this nor Plume's rather explicit reply are at all changed. Furthermore, the passage substituted is clearly better: it involves all four characters on stage in tense interplay, full of amusing ironies that only Silvia and the audience can appreciate.

The first version of the other re-written passage, in Act II, scene i, reads:

SILVIA
Sir, you're welcome to England.

PLUME
Blessings in heaven we should receive in a prostrate posture, let me receive my welcome thus.   *Kneels and kisses her hand*

SILVIA
Pray rise, sir, I'll give you fair quarter.

PLUME
All quarter I despise, the height of conquest is to die at your feet.
          Kissing her hand again

SILVIA
Well, well, you shall die at my feet, or where you will; but first let

---

me desire you to make your will, perhaps you'll leave me something.[10]

Plume's first speech here might have been rejected as too profane; more probably this happened because the kneeling business was so inept; and the only line preserved in the second version was the highly improper 'you shall die at my feet, or where you will'. Again, the later version is much longer, and tougher in texture. Silvia's comment, 'I have often heard that soldiers were sincere' is a jest about the theatrical stereotype of the bluff soldier going a-wooing, not, as Shugrue thinks, something 'clearly designed to improve the public image of soldiers'.[11] In short, the two new passages are manifestly Farquhar's, and dramatically superior to those they replace.

The three important omissions in Q2 are the song from Act III, scene i, the devil's-hand-gripping incident from Act IV, scene ii, and the whole of Act V, scene i. The song 'Come, fair one, be kind', was sung in the earliest performances, as is evident from the title of the broadsheet publication (see Appendix 2 below); yet, it is dramatically extraneous, and the words at best mediocre. It was probably not well enough liked to have lasting-power. I tend to agree with Archer's opinion that the hand-gripping passage is 'outrageously farcical'; it is difficult to stage (Plume has to creep in from off-stage, or from behind a screen, and reach under the table, then return, all without being seen by Melinda and Lucy), and it is out of character with the rest of the scene, for which reason I exclude it from my text. Perhaps Farquhar thought, like Chaves in 1705, that 'nought but Farce and Song can please the Age',[12] and provided enough of either to help his play survive the difficult first night. The first scene in Act V is an amusing, mildly improper sequence of a mere 37 lines. It may have been cut to please the censor, yet it is not necessary to the progress of the various actions, and its one really good line, Rose's 'I don't know whether I had a bedfellow or not', is repeated in scene vii.

The present edition is based on Q1 (taking as copy-text British Museum, 11773.g.11), with the adoption of those Q2 revisions considered to be Farquhar's, to produce a text which, as far as one may judge, corresponds to his latest intentions. Some passages omitted in Q2 are, however, retained, for their intrinsic interest, with an appropriate note, where this can be done without harm to the general character of the scene or context.

---

[10] Replaced by the present edition's lines 50–64; accidentals modernized.
[11] Shugrue, p. xi.
[12] Nicoll, p. 10.

A simplified pattern has been imposed upon scene headings, and scene numbers, which are not present in the quartos, are supplied in black letter. Round brackets are employed, where necessary, to distinguish original stage directions from dialogue, and square brackets, those which are editorial. The direction *Aside* has been placed before the speech to which it refers, lineated with the dialogue when it applies to only part of a speech, otherwise with the speech prefix. Spelling has been modernized in accordance with the conventions of this series.

INTRODUCTORY NOTE TO THE REVISED EDITION

Since 1977 the play has been admirably edited by Peter Dixon (Revels Plays series, 1986) and Shirley Strum Kenny (within the Clarendon Press's *The Works of George Farquhar*, 1988). While the scale of their annotation and textual apparatus exceeds what would be appropriate for the New Mermaid series, I welcome the opportunity to remedy deficiencies revealed in my own work.

Both editors argue convincingly that the play's second quarto edition (Q2) had as its copy-text not a marked-up copy of Q1, as I had contended, but a separate manuscript. Kenny believes it was probably the playhouse prompt-book (p. 23). Dixon contends that it was a copy made for the publisher (by 'a scribe of pedantic disposition') of the 'fair version' which Farquhar had prepared for the playhouse, duly 'cut and altered' to keep it in compliance with the prompt-book, but not itself that prompt-book (otherwise the II.iii speech-prefix confusion would have been cleared up, and some exit directions provided for servants) (pp. 35–40). Kenny and Dixon both stress the 'reformation of manners' pressure *ca.* 1706, to censor theatre-scripts of immorality or blasphemy.

The effect of both hypotheses is to strengthen the case for preserving the readings of the Q1 version, except where Q2's revisions are manifestly authorial and introduced solely for their greater dramatic and stylistic merits. The Q1 passages from II.i and IV.ii, relegated, as A(i) and A(iii) (a) and (b), to my Appendix 1 (pp. 127–8), could well be incorporated within the text.

It may be re-emphasized that my textual footnotes do not list fully Q1/Q2 variations, but only those instances where Q2's variant has replaced Q1's, with Q1 as general copy-text.

The time the play was written remains uncertain, but R. J. Jordan considers that Farquhar's recruiting activities in England for the Earl of Orrery's Regiment probably took him to Shrewsbury for part of the time between 14 June and 20 October 1704, rather than for later drives between November 1704 and March 1705, and after 25 October 1705 ('George Farquhar's Military Career', *Huntington Library Quarterly*, XXVII [1974], 251–64). If the tradition about his writing the play while staying in the town has some truth in it, he may have drafted part of it, at least, in the summer of 1704, and completed it in late 1705–early 1706.

The date of publication can be pushed back to on or before 25 April 1706, when the *Daily Courant* advertises 'There is now published, The Recruiting Officer, . . .' (see my p. xxxiv).

'E. Blakeway' (p. xvi) was the Reverend Edward Blakeway, minister of St. Mary's, Shrewsbury (from 1763), the rector of Long Staunton (from 1764), and his informant was his aunt, Anne Blakeway, who died in February 1766. Her identifications of the originals for characters first appeared in print 'in a set of "Additional Notes" appended to volume one of the 1786 edition of *The Tatler*', on p. 425 (Bertram H. Davis, 'Thomas Percy and *The Recruiting Officer*,' *N & Q*, n.s. XXX [1983], 490–1). The letter of 4 July 1765 was reprinted in John Nichols' *Illustrations of the Literary History of the Eighteenth Century*, V (1828), 643–5. For further biographical details about the people identified, see my 'Some Notes . . .' (Further Reading).

FURTHER READING

Anselment, Raymond A., ed., *George Farquhar: 'The Recruiting Officer' and 'The Beaux' Stratagem'. A Casebook,* London, 1977.

Brown, Laura, *English Dramatic Form, 1660–1760*: An Essay in Dramatic History, New Haven & London, 1981.

Burns, Edward, *Restoration Comedy: Crises of Desire and Identity,* Basingstoke, 1987.

Connely, Willard, *Young George Farquhar. The Restoration Drama at Twilight,* New York, 1930.

Dixon, Peter, ed., *The Recruiting Officer* (Revels Plays series), Manchester, 1986.

Hume, Robert D., *The Development of English Drama in the Late Seventeenth Century,* Oxford, 1976.

James, Eugene Nelson, *The Development of George Farquhar as a Comic Dramatist,* The Hague, 1972.

—— *George Farquhar: A Reference Guide,* Boston, Mass., 1986.

Kenneally, Thomas, *The Playmaker,* London, etc, 1987. [Novel about production of this play by convicts at Sydney Cove, Australia.]

Kenny, Shirley Strum, *The Works of George Farquhar,* 2 vols., Oxford, 1988.

Loftis, J., Southern, R., Jones, M., and Scouten, A. H.., *The Revels History of Drama in English,* vol. V, *1600–1750,* London, 1976.

Loftis, John, *Comedy and Society from Congreve to Fielding,* Stanford, California, 1959.

Pearson, Jacqueline, *The Prostituted Muse: Images of Women and Women Dramatists 1642–1737,* New York, London, [etc.], 1988.

Rosenfeld, Sybil, 'Notes on *The Recruiting Officer', Theatre Notebook,* XVIII (1963–64), 47–8.

Ross, J. C., 'Some Notes on *The Recruiting Officer', N & Q,* n.s. XVIII (1981), 216–21.

Rothstein, Eric, *George Farquhar* (Twayne's English Authors series), New York, 1967.

Schneider, Ben Ross, Jr., *The Ethos of Restoration Comedy,* Urbana, Illinois, 1971.

Scouller, R. E. *The Armies of Queen Anne,* Oxford, 1966.

Sharma, R. C., *Themes and Conventions of the Comedy of Manners,* New Delhi, 1965.

Smith, John Harrington, *The Gay Couple in Restoration Comedy,* Cambridge, Mass., 1948.

Stafford-Clark, Max, *Letters to George: The Account of a Rehearsal,*
    London 1989. [Progress reports on rehearsals of *The Recruiting Officer,*
    and on the genesis of Timberlake Wertenbaker's companion piece *Our
    Country's Good,* about transported convicts involved in the production
    Kenneally writes about.]
Wertheim, Albert, 'Bertolt Brecht and George Farquhar's *The Recruiting
    Officer*', *Comparative Drama,* VII (1973), 179–90.

THE
Recruiting Officer.

A
COMEDY.

As it is Acted at the

THEATRE ROYAL

IN

DRURY-LANE,

By Her MAJESTY's Servants.

Written by Mr. FARQUHAR.

—— *Captique Æolis, donisque coacti.*
Virg. Lib. II. Æneid.

LONDON:

Printed for BERNARD LINTOTT at the *Cross Keys* next
Nando's Coffee-House near *Temple-Bar.*

Price 1 *s.* 6 *d.*

Æolis properly, *dolis* (so corrected, Q1 errata)

Captique dolis, donisque coacti. 'Captured with tricks and brought together with (or, urged on by) gifts', adapted from Virgil's *Æneid*, II, 196: *captique dolis lacrimisque coactis*, 'captured with tricks and forced tears'. Rothstein (p. 133) perceives an ingenious reversal of the situation of the fall of Troy. Since England must avoid like consequences of 'foolish trust and disarmament', Kite's stratagems to enlist defenders receive some degree of justification. On another plane, 'the heroic comparison between beleaguered Troy and beleaguered Tummas Appletree is so grotesque as to indicate Farquhar's limited sympathy for the victims of recruitment'.

EPISTLE DEDICATORY
To All Friends Round the Wrekin

My Lords and Gentlemen,
   Instead of the mercenary expectations that attend addresses
of this nature, I humbly beg, that this may be received as an
acknowledgment for the favours you have already conferred.
I have transgressed the rules of dedication in offering you   5
anything in that style without first asking your leave; but the
entertainment I found in Shropshire commands me to be
grateful, and that's all I intend.
   'Twas my good fortune to be ordered some time ago into the
place which is made the scene of this comedy; I was a perfect   10
stranger to everything in Salop, but its character of loyalty, the
number of its inhabitants, the alacrity of the gentlemen in
recruiting the army, with their generous and hospitable
reception of strangers.
   This character I found so amply verified in every particular,   15
that you made recruiting, which is the greatest fatigue upon
earth to others, to be the greatest pleasure in the world to me.
   The kingdom cannot show better bodies of men, better
inclinations for the service, more generosity, more good understanding, nor more politeness, than is to be found at the foot of   20
the Wrekin.
   Some little turns of humour that I met with almost within

0.–1, 21, 65 *Wrekin* Q1 errata (Rekin Q1) a dominating, isolated hill,
   1,335 feet high, about ten miles to the east of Shrewsbury
7 *entertainment* reception, treatment.
11 *Salop* Shropshire, also Shrewsbury.

1–8 Authors customarily dedicated their works to wealthy individuals,
   first asking their permission, in hope of a gift of guineas, and, maybe,
   longer-term patronage. Farquhar affects to believe that dedications, like
   plays, should conform to classical 'rules'.

the shade of that famous hill gave the rise to this comedy; and
people were apprehensive, that, by the example of some others,
I would make the town merry at the expense of the country   25
gentlemen. But they forgot that I was to write a comedy, not a
libel; and that whilst I held to nature, no person of any
character in your country could suffer by being exposed. I have
drawn the justice and the clown in their *puris naturalibus*: the
one an apprehensive, sturdy, brave blockhead; and the other a   30
worthy, honest, generous gentleman, hearty in his country's
cause, and of as good an understanding as I could give him,
which I must confess is far short of his own.

I humbly beg leave to interline a word or two of the adventures of *The Recruiting Officer* upon the stage. Mr Rich, who   35
commands the company for which those recruits were raised,
has desired me to acquit him before the world of a charge
which he thinks lies heavy upon him for acting this play on
Mr Durfey's third night.

Be it known unto all men by these presents, that it was my   40
act and deed, or rather Mr Durfey's; for he *would* play his third
night against the first of mine. He brought down a huge flight
of frightful birds upon me, when, heaven knows, I had not a
feathered fowl in my play except one single Kite; but I

---

23 *rise* origin   25 *country* county
29 *puris naturalibus* natural state
30 *apprehensive* 'quick on the uptake', possessing mother wit
34 *interline* interpolate
40 *these presents* these words, the present document (legal)

23–33 Farquhar here signals 'a major shift in attitude, away from the
   traditional contempt for the squirearchy' (Loftis, p. 72), found in
   nearly all Restoration comedy, and exemplified in Congreve's portrayal
   of Sir Wilfull Witwoud, who is made to come from Shropshire, near
   Shrewsbury, in *The Way of the World* (1700).
35 *Mr Rich.* Christopher Rich (d. 1714), patentee and manager of the
   Theatre Royal, Drury Lane, between 1688 and 1709, notoriously auto-
   cratic towards his actors.
39 *Mr Durfey's third night.* Thomas Durfey's first author's-benefit performance for his comic opera, *Wonders in the Sun; or, The Kingdom of
   the Birds*, which had opened at the rival theatre, the Queen's in the
   Haymarket, on Friday 5 April. Dramatists' incomes largely depended
   on the profits of benefit performances, and the clash left him with a
   sadly thin audience. His opera closed after five nights, earning less than
   half its production costs (Nicoll, p. 233).
42–3 *huge . . . birds.* Durfey's cast included many strange birds, represented by elaborately costumed actors, or painted figures.

presently made Plume a bird, because of his name, and Brazen   45
another, because of the feather in his hat; and with these three
I engaged his whole empire, which I think was as great a *wonder*
as any *in the sun*.

But to answer his complaints more gravely, the season was
far advanced; the officers that made the greatest figures in my   50
play were all commanded to their posts abroad, and waited only
for a wind, which might possibly turn in less time than a day;
and I know none of Mr Durfey's birds that had posts abroad
but his woodcocks, and their season is over; so that he might
put off a day with less prejudice than the *Recruiting Officer*   55
could, who has this farther to say for himself, that he was
posted before the other spoke, and could not with credit recede
from his station.

These and some other rubs this comedy met with before it
appeared. But on the other hand, it had powerful helps to set it   60
forward: the Duke of Ormonde encouraged the author, and the
Earl of Orrery approved the play. My recruits were reviewed

---

57 *posted* (a) appointed to his command, or place of duty; (b) advertised, by sticking play-bills on posts
59 *rubs* hindrances, difficulties

49–50 *the season was far advanced.* (a) The campaigning season in Flanders
began in spring: 'the Battle of Ramillies was fought just six weeks after
the first night of the play' (Archer); (b) the theatrical season ran till
July, but contained limited provision for new works.

54 *woodcocks.* Dixon notes that 'The woodcock winters in the British Isles,
notably in Ireland, and returns to Scandinavia in the very early spring'; so
by April 'Its shooting season [was] over'. Though Durfey's *dramatis
personae* did not contain this bird, Prelate Magpie is 'Abbot of Buzzard-
land and Woodcocks'. Fig., fools, simpletons.

61 *the Duke of Ormonde.* James Butler (1665–1745), 2nd Duke, appointed
Lord-Lieutenant of Ireland in 1703, and in 1702, General of the Horse.
He had approved Farquhar's lieutenancy, and gave him kind words, but
neither financial help nor further promotion. He had reviewed
Farquhar's regiment, among others, in Dublin on 26 March 1705
(Jordan, p. 258).

61–2 *the Earl of Orrery.* Charles Boyle (1676–1731), 4th Earl, who in 1704
gave Farquhar a commission as lieutenant of grenadiers in his new
regiment. He was himself author of a manners-comedy, *As You Find It*
(1703).

by my general and my colonel, and could not fail to pass muster, and still to add to my success, they were raised among my friends round the Wrekin. 65

'This Health has the advantage over our other celebrated toasts, never to grow worse for the wearing; 'tis a lasting beauty, old without age and common without scandal. That you may live long to set it cheerfully round, and to enjoy the abundant pleasures of your fair and plentiful country, is the 70 hearty wish of,

My Lords and Gentlemen,
Your most obliged,
and most obedient servant,
Geo. Farquhar. 75

66 *This Health* i.e., this toast of 'good health'

63–4 *pass muster* Soldiers could fail to pass muster if found at the muster parade to be absent, passing under false names, or physically inadequate (R.E. Scouller, *The Armies of Queen Anne*, Oxford, 1966, pp. 133–5).

67 *toasts* (a) salutations wishing health: 'To all friends round the Wrekin' was a well-known Shropshire toast; (b) ladies nominated as persons to whose health the company is to drink (cf. *Tatler,* Nos 24, 31). 'The health suddenly became a popular sub-genre [of verse] during the election of 1705', mostly through the efforts of high church Tory writers (*Poems on Affairs of State: Augustan Satirical Verse, 1660–1714,* ed. G. de F. Lord *et al,* 7 vols [New Haven & London, 1963–75], VII, 60).

THE PROLOGUE

In ancient times, when Helen's fatal charms
Roused the contending universe to arms,
The Grecian council happily deputes
The sly Ulysses forth – to raise recruits.
The artful captain found, without delay,   5
Where great Achilles, a deserter, lay.
Him Fate had warned to shun the Trojan blows;
Him Greece required – against their Trojan foes.
All the recruiting arts were needful here
To raise this great, this tim'rous volunteer.   10
Ulysses well could talk – he stirs, he warms
The warlike youth. He listens to the charms
Of plunder, fine laced coats, and glitt'ring arms.
Ulysses caught the young aspiring boy,
And listed him who wrought the fate of Troy.   15
Thus by recruiting was bold Hector slain;
Recruiting thus fair Helen did regain.
If for one Helen such prodigious things
Were acted, that they even listed kings;
If for one Helen's artful, vicious charms,   20
Half the transported world was found in arms;

11 *warms* Q2 (warns Q1) renders eager, exhorts to valour
15 *listed* enlisted

1–15 Achilles' goddess-mother Thetis learnt that he was fated to a life
either long and obscure, or glorious but brief, and had him hidden on
the island of Scyros, in woman's clothes. The seer Calchas prophesied
that Troy could not be taken without Achilles' help. Verbal echoes
identify the source from which Farquhar took the story of how Ulysses
set off to find him, and recruited him, as Sir Robert Howard's verse
translation of Statius' *Achilleis*, printed in Howard's *Poems* (1660),
pp. 222–59, and *Poems on Several Occasions* (1696), pp. 171–282.

What for so many Helens may we dare,
Whose minds, as well as faces, are so fair?
If, by one Helen's eyes, old Greece could find
Its Homer fired to write – even Homer blind,   25
The Britons sure beyond compare may write,
That view so many Helens every night.

22–3 Ian Donaldson has suggested that these lines allude to the importance of the presence of women and military officers in the first audiences, which 'may have had some effect on the design of the play as a whole' (review of Jeffares, *N&Q*, ccxx (1975), 516–18).

DRAMATIS PERSONAE

Men

MR BALANCE ⎫	*Mr Keen*
MR SCALE ⎬ *three Justices*	*Mr Phillips*
MR SCRUPLE ⎭	*Mr Kent*
MR WORTHY, *a gentleman of Shropshire*	*Mr Williams*
CAPTAIN PLUME, *a recruiting officer*	*Mr Wilks*
CAPTAIN BRAZEN, *a recruiting officer*	*Mr Cibber*
KITE, *Sergeant to Plume*	*Mr Estcourt*
BULLOCK, *a country clown*	*Mr Bullock*
COSTAR PEARMAIN, *a recruit*	*Mr Norris*
THOMAS APPLETREE, *a recruit*	*Mr Fairbank*
[PLUCK, *a butcher*]	
[THOMAS, *a smith*]	
[BRIDEWELL, *a constable*]	

Women

MELINDA, *a lady of fortune*	*Mrs Rogers*
SILVIA, *daughter to Balance, in love with Plume*	*Mrs Oldfield*
LUCY, *Melinda's maid*	*Mrs Sapsford*
ROSE, *a country wench*	*Mrs Mountfort*

Recruits, [drummer,] mob, servants and attendants

Scene *Shrewsbury*

COSTAR PEARMAIN Both names denote varieties of apples, the costar, or
    costard, being especially large.

9

THE RECRUITING OFFICER

Act I, Scene i

The Market-place
DRUMMER *beats the 'Grenadier March'*
Enter SERGEANT KITE, *followed by the* MOB

KITE (*Making a speech*)
  If any gentlemen soldiers, or others, have a mind to serve
  Her Majesty, and pull down the French king; if any prentices
  have severe masters, any children have undutiful parents; if
  any servants have too little wages, or any husband too much
  wife; let them repair to the noble Sergeant Kite, at the Sign   5
  of the Raven, in this good town of Shrewsbury, and they shall
  receive present relief and entertainment. – Gentlemen, I
  don't beat my drums here to ensnare or inveigle any man;
  for you must know, gentlemen, that I am a man of honour.
  Besides, I don't beat up for common soldiers; no, I list only   10
  grenadiers, grenadiers, gentlemen – pray, gentlemen, observe
  this cap – this is the cap of honour, it dubs a man a gentleman in the drawing of a tricker; and he that has the good
  fortune to be born six foot high was born to be a great man.
  (*To one of the Mob*) Sir, will you give me leave to try this cap   15
  upon your head?

0.2 s.d. DRUMMER Ed. (*Drum* Q; i.e., Drummer)
5–6 *the Sign of the Raven* the Raven Hotel, in Castle Street
12 *cap* special headwear of grenadier troops, narrow, with a tall,
   mitre-shaped front
13 *tricker* trigger; 'in . . . tricker': instantly

0.2–0.3 s.d. *'The* MOB' (*mobile*, crowd), lower-class townspeople and
   countrymen, includes Costar Pearmain and Thomas Appletree. Later
   C18 editions make the entry quasi-processional: '*Enter* Drummer,
   beating the "Grenadier's March", Serjeant Kite, Costar Pearmain,
   Thomas Appletree, *and* Mob'.
0.2 *Drum* (Q reading) may mean drum 'beating offstage' (Dixon).
   Grenadier March Printed first in *A Collection of the Newest and Choicest
   Songs*, 1683. See Appendix 2.
11 *grenadiers*. Specialist grenade-throwing infantry, chosen for height and
   strength. At this time they formed a separate company within each foot
   regiment, and served as assault troops in siege or trench warfare.

MOB

Is there no harm in't? Won't the cap list me?

KITE

No, no, no more than I can, – come, let me see how it
becomes you.

MOB

Are you sure there be no conjuration in it, no gunpowder   20
plot upon me?

KITE

No, no, friend; don't fear, man.

MOB

My mind misgives me plaguily – let me see it. (*Going to put
it on*) It smells woundily of sweat and brimstone; pray,
Sergeant, what writing is this upon the face of it?   25

KITE

'The Crown, or the Bed of Honour'.

MOB

Pray now, what may be that same bed of honour?

KITE

Oh, a mighty large bed, bigger by half than the great bed of
Ware, ten thousand people may lie in't together and never
feel one another.   30

---

20 *conjuration* magic spell, conjuring
23 *plaguily* Q2 (plaguely Q1) confoundedly
24 *woundily* dreadfully, excessively
26 *the Bed of Honour* (death on) the field of battle

---

17 s.p. MOB i.e., one of the mob. Later C18 editions identify him with
Costar Pearmain, which may have been Farquhar's final intention. It
reflects stage-tradition, and improves dramatic continuity between
I.i and II.iii. He sounds however more like a townsman.

26 *The Crown . . . Honour* Grenadier caps generally bore, on the stiff
front, the crown and the royal cipher, or else the motto of the regiment's
colonel. No trace has been found of this particular motto's having
been associated with any British regiment; apparently it was Farquhar's
invention, or a professional jest.

28–9 *the great bed of Ware*. A handsome, carved four-poster, first made
famous while in the Crown Inn (some authorities say, the Saracen's
Head) at Ware, Hertfordshire, and now in the Victoria and Albert
Museum. It measures 10 feet 8½ inches wide, 11 feet 1 inch deep, and
was made between 1575 and 1600, though it bears the date '1460'.
Literary references to it include those in *Twelfth Night* and Jonson's
Silent Woman. (See Lawrence Wright, *Warm and Snug: the History of
the Bed* [1962], pp. 69–70.)

MOB

My wife and I would do well to lie in't, for we don't care for feeling one another – but do folk sleep sound in this same bed of honour?

KITE

Sound! Aye, so sound that they never wake.

MOB

Wauns! I wish again that my wife lay there.   35

KITE

Say you so? Then I find, brother –

MOB

Brother! Hold there, friend, I'm no kindred to you that I know of, as yet – look'ee, Sergeant, no coaxing, no wheedling, d'ye see; if I have a mind to list, why so – if not, why 'tis not so – therefore take your cap and your brothership back   40 again, for I an't disposed at this present writing – no coaxing, no brothering me, faith.

KITE

I coax! I wheedle! I'm above it. Sir, I have served twenty campaigns. But sir, you talk well, and I must own that you are a man every inch of you, a pretty, young, sprightly   45 fellow – I love a fellow with a spirit, but I scorn to coax, 'tis base; though I must say that never in my life have I seen a man better built; how firm and strong he treads, he steps like a castle! But I scorn to wheedle any man – come, honest lad, will you take share of a pot?   50

MOB

Nay, for that matter, I'll spend my penny with the best he that wears a head, that is, begging your pardon, sir, and in a fair way.

KITE

Give me your hand then; and now, gentlemen, I have no more to say but this – here's a purse of gold, and there is a   55 tub of humming ale at my quarters; 'tis the Queen's money and the Queen's drink. She's a generous queen and loves her subjects – I hope, gentlemen, you won't refuse the Queen's health?

35 *Wauns* dialect-form of 'Wounds', a mild oath; from 'God's wounds'
38 *look'ee* Q2 (lookye Q1)
38 *coaxing* includes sense 'persuading by flattery'
42 *faith* in faith, i.e., in truth
48 *man better built* Q2 (better built man Q1)
56 *humming* strong, frothing(?)

ALL MOB

No, no, no.   60

KITE

Huzza then! Huzza for the Queen, and the honour of
Shropshire!

ALL MOB

Huzza!

KITE

Beat drum.

Exeunt, drummer beating the 'Grenadier March'

Enter PLUME *in a riding habit*

PLUME

By the Grenadier March that should be my drum, and by that   65
shout it should beat with success – let me see – (*looks on his
watch*) – four o'clock – at ten yesterday morning I left
London – a hundred and twenty miles in thirty hours is
pretty smart riding, but nothing to the fatigue of recruiting.

Enter KITE

KITE

Welcome to Shrewsbury, noble Captain: from the banks of   70
the Danube to the Severn side, noble Captain, you're
welcome.

PLUME

A very elegant reception indeed, Mr Kite, I find you are
fairly entered into your recruiting strain – pray, what
success?   75

KITE

I have been here but a week and I have recruited five.

PLUME

Five! Pray, what are they?

KITE

I have listed the strong man of Kent, the king of the gypsies,

64 s.d. *drummer* Ed. (*drum* Q)
71 *you're* Q2 (you are Q1)

70–1 *from . . . side* Plume is supposed to have recently returned from the
Battle of Blenheim, fought beside the Danube.
78 *the strong man of Kent*. William Joy, or Joyce, the Kentish strong man,
known as the Southwark Samson (Ashton, p. 201). He had aroused
Farquhar's resentment in late 1699 when he had hired the disused
Dorset Gardens playhouse for exhibitions of 'dexterities of strength',
competing for audiences with the first run of *The Constant Couple* (see
its prologue, ll. 32–9, in Stonehill, I, 87–8; *The London Stage, 1660–
1800*, Part 1, pp. 517, 518, 520).

a Scotch pedlar, a scoundrel attorney, and a Welsh parson.

PLUME

An attorney! Wert thou mad? List a lawyer! Discharge him,   80
discharge him this minute.

KITE

Why, sir?

PLUME

Because I will have nobody in my company that can write;
a fellow that can write, can draw petitions – I say, this
minute discharge him.   85

KITE

And what shall I do with the parson?

PLUME

Can he write?

KITE

Umh – he plays rarely upon the fiddle.

PLUME

Keep him by all means. But how stands the country affected?
Were the people pleased with the news of my coming to   90
town?

KITE

Sir, the mob are so pleased with your honour, and the
justices and better sort of people are so delighted with me,
that we shall soon do our business. But, sir, you have got a
recruit here that you little think of.   95

PLUME

Who?

KITE

One that you beat up for last time you were in the country:
You remember your old friend Molly at the Castle?

PLUME

She's not with child, I hope.

KITE

No, no, sir; she was brought to bed yesterday.   100

PLUME

Kite, you must father the child.

KITE

Humph – and so her friends will oblige me to marry the
mother.

102 *friends* relations (as well as modern sense)

98 *the Castle.* Shrewsbury Castle (map, Appendix 3), built in the C13,
had lost its status as a royal fortress during the reign of Charles II, and
its use was residential only.

PLUME

If they should, we'll take her with us, she can wash, you
know, and make a bed upon occasion.   105

KITE

Aye, or unmake it upon occasion. But your honour knows
that I'm married already.

PLUME

To how many?

KITE

I can't tell readily – I have set them down here upon the back
of the muster-roll. (*Draws it out*) Let me see – *Imprimis*,   110
Mrs Sheely Snickereyes, she sells potatoes upon Ormonde
Quay in Dublin – Peggy Guzzle, the brandy-woman at the
Horse-guard at Whitehall – Dolly Waggon, the carrier's
daughter in Hull – Mademoiselle Van-bottom-flat at the
Buss – then Jenny Oakum, the ship-carpenter's widow at   115
Portsmouth; but I don't reckon upon her, for she was
married at the same time to two lieutenants of marines, and
a man of war's boatswain.

PLUME

A full company – you have named five – come, make 'em half
a dozen, Kite. Is the child a boy or a girl?   120

KITE

A chopping boy.

PLUME

Then set the mother down in your list, and the boy in mine;
enter him a grenadier by the name of Francis Kite, absent
upon furlough – I'll allow you a man's pay for his sub-

104 *they* Q2 (she Q1)
110 s.d. *Draws it out* Q2 (*Draws out the Muster-roll* Q1)
     Imprimis in the first place
115 *the Buss* 's Hertogenbosch, in North Brabant, Holland
121 *chopping* big and vigorous

---

113 *Horse-Guard* barracks and stables for the Horse Guards, in Whitehall.
122–4 *set . . . furlough.* J. Burton Hill has drawn attention to an instance
     illustrating the practice of the day, in a letter from the Secretary of War
     to the Paymaster-General dated 28 September 1711: 'Her Majesty
     having been pleased to grant Fitton Minshull, a child, a commission of
     Ensign in Brigadier Stanwix's Regiment of Foot, in order for the sup-
     port of his mother and family . . . has likewise given him a furlough to be
     absent from his duty until further notice' (from Charles M. Clode,
     The Military Forces of the Crown; their Administration and Government
     [1869], II, 610; cited in Hill's *A History of the Reign of Queen Anne*
     [1880], I, 205).   124–5 *subsistence* See Appendix 5.

sistence; and now go comfort the wench in the straw.   125
KITE
I shall, sir.
PLUME
But hold, have you made any use of your German doctor's
habit since you arrived?
KITE
Yes, yes, sir; and my fame's all about the country for the
most faithful fortune-teller that ever told a lie; I was obliged   130
to let my landlord into the secret for the convenience of
keeping it so, but he's an honest fellow and will be trusty to
any roguery that is confided to him. This device, sir, will get
you men, and me money, which I think is all we want at
present – but yonder comes your friend Mr Worthy – has   135
your honour any farther commands?
PLUME
None at present.   *Exit* KITE
'Tis indeed the picture of Worthy, but the life's departed.

Enter WORTHY

PLUME
What, arms a-cross, Worthy! Methinks you should hold 'em
open when a friend's so near. The man has got the vapours   140
in his ears, I believe; I must expel this melancholy spirit.
     Spleen, thou worst of fiends below,
     Fly, I conjure thee by this magic blow.
                         Slaps WORTHY *on the shoulder*
WORTHY
Plume! My dear Captain, welcome. Safe and sound returned!
PLUME
I 'scaped safe from Germany, and sound, I hope, from   145
London: you see I have lost neither leg, arm nor nose; then
for my inside, 'tis neither troubled with sympathies nor
antipathies, and I have an excellent stomach for roast beef.

125 *in the straw* in her lying-in
130 *faithful* Q2 (famous Q1) veracious
145 *sound* uninfected with syphilis, which caused decay of the nose
148 *stomach* appetite

---

140 *the vapours.* Exhalations supposedly developed within the bodily
     organs; or, the morbid condition caused by them.
142 *Spleen.* Excessive dejection of spirits, gloominess, and irritability;
     melancholia.
147–8 *sympathies nor antipathies.* Excessive affinities, or contrarieties,
     between the different bodily organs, promoting and spreading disorders.

WORTHY

Thou art a happy fellow; once I was so.

PLUME

What ails thee, man? No inundations nor earthquakes in   150
Wales, I hope? Has your father rose from the dead, and
reassumed his estate?

WORTHY

No.

PLUME

Then you are married, surely.

WORTHY

No.   155

PLUME

Then you are mad, or turning Quaker.

WORTHY

Come, I must out with it – your once gay, roving friend is
dwindled into an obsequious, thoughtful, romantic, constant
coxcomb.

PLUME

And pray, what is all this for?   160

WORTHY

For a woman.

PLUME

Shake hands, brother, if you go to that – behold me as
obsequious, as thoughtful, and as constant a coxcomb as
your worship.

WORTHY

For whom?   165

PLUME

For a regiment. – But for a woman! 'Sdeath! I have been
constant to fifteen at a time, but never melancholy for one;
and can the love of one bring you into this pickle? Pray, who
is this miraculous Helen?

WORTHY

A Helen indeed, not to be won under a ten years' siege; as   170
great a beauty, and as great a jilt.

PLUME

A jilt! Pho! Is she as great a whore?

158 *thoughtful* moody

---

156 *Quaker*. Ashton (p. 351) notices 'an insane dislike to Quakers in Queen
Anne's reign'; Quaker sobriety was associated inevitably with fanatic
enthusiasm and dishonesty.

WORTHY

No, no.

PLUME

'Tis ten thousand pities; but who is she? Do I know her?

WORTHY

Very well.   175

PLUME

Impossible! – I know no woman that will hold out a ten
years' siege.

WORTHY

What think you of Melinda?

PLUME

Melinda! Why, she began to capitulate this time twelve-
month, and offered to surrender upon honourable terms;   180
and I advised you to propose a settlement of five hundred
pound a year to her, before I went last abroad.

WORTHY

I did, and she hearkened to't, desiring only one week to
consider; when beyond her hopes the town was relieved, and
I forced to turn my siege into a blockade.   185

PLUME

Explain, explain.

WORTHY

My Lady Richly, her aunt in Flintshire, dies, and leaves her
at this critical time twenty thousand pound.

PLUME

Oh, the devil! What a delicate woman was there spoiled! But
by the rules of war now, Worthy, blockade was foolish –   190
after such a convoy of provisions was entered the place, you
could have no thought of reducing it by famine – you should
have redoubled your attacks, taken the town by storm, or
have died upon the breach.

WORTHY

I did make one general assault, and pushed it with all my   195
forces; but I was so vigorously repulsed, that despairing of
ever gaining her for a mistress, I have altered my conduct,
given my addresses the obsequious and distant turn, and
court her now for a wife.

179 *capitulate* negotiate, parley
190 *blockade* Q2 (your blockade Q1)

194 *died upon the breach.* Libertine equivoque for premature ejaculation;
    cf. Etherege's 'The Imperfect Enjoyment'.

PLUME

So, as you grew obsequious, she grew haughty, and because   200
you approached her as a goddess, she used you like a dog.

WORTHY

Exactly.

PLUME

'Tis the way of 'em all. Come, Worthy, your obsequious and
distant airs will never bring you together; you must not think
to surmount her pride by your humility. Would you bring   205
her to better thoughts of you, she must be reduced to a
meaner opinion of herself – let me see – the very first thing
that I would do, should be to lie with her chambermaid, and
hire three or four wenches in the neighbourhood to report
that I had got them with child. Suppose we lampooned all   210
the pretty women in town, and left her out? Or what if we
made a ball, and forgot to invite her, with one or two of the
ugliest?

WORTHY

These would be mortifications, I must confess; but we live in
such a precise, dull place that we can have no balls, no   215
lampoons, no –

PLUME

What! No bastards! And so many recruiting officers in
town; I thought 'twas a maxim among them to leave as many
recruits in the country as they carried out.

WORTHY

Nobody doubts your goodwill, noble Captain, in serving your   220
country with your best blood: witness our friend Molly at
the Castle, – there have been tears in town about that
business, Captain.

PLUME

I hope Silvia has not heard of't.

WORTHY

Oh sir, have you thought of her? I began to fancy you had   225
forgot poor Silvia.

---

201 *used . . . dog* proverbial. Tilley D 514
215 *precise* puritanical

215–16 *no . . . lampoons.* Gaskill's National Theatre production made the
    double entendre explicit by inserting Plume's astonished 'What?' before
    'no lampoons' (Tynan). It was probably intentional already.
220–1 *serving . . . blood.* Probably alluding to the notion that intercourse
    involved a small blood-loss, cf. Donne's 'The Flea'; otherwise, blood:
    mettle.

PLUME

Your affairs had put mine quite out of my head. 'Tis true,
Silvia and I had once agreed to go to bed together, could we
have adjusted preliminaries; but she would have the
wedding before consummation, and I was for consum-   230
mation before the wedding – we could not agree. She was a
pert obstinate fool, and would lose her maidenhead her own
way, so she may keep it for Plume.

WORTHY

But do you intend to marry upon no other conditions?

PLUME

Your pardon, sir, I'll marry upon no condition at all, – if I   235
should, I'm resolved never to bind myself to a woman for my
whole life, till I know whether I shall like her company for
half an hour. Suppose I married a woman that wanted a leg?
Such a thing might be, unless I examined the goods beforehand. If people would but try one another's constitutions   240
before they engaged, it would prevent all these elopements,
divorces, and the devil knows what.

WORTHY

Nay, for that matter, the town did not stick to say, that –

PLUME

I hate country towns for that reason – if your town has a
dishonourable thought of Silvia, it deserves to be burnt to   245
the ground. – I love Silvia, I admire her frank, generous
disposition; there's something in that girl more than woman,
her sex is but a foil to her – the ingratitude, dissimulation,
envy, pride, avarice, and vanity of her sister females, do but
set off their contraries in her – in short, were I once a   250
general, I would marry her.

WORTHY

Faith, you have reason; for were you but a corporal, she
would marry you. But my Melinda coquettes it with every
fellow she sees – I lay fifty pound she makes love to you.

PLUME

I'll lay fifty pound that I return it if she does – look'ee,   255
Worthy, I'll win her and give her to you afterwards.

227 *mine* Q2 (my own Q1)
233 *for Plume* i.e., with no opposition from me
235 *condition* Q2 (conditions Q1)
240 *constitutions* 'temperaments; often explicitly inclinations' (Dixon)
241 *engaged* (a) embarked on business venture; (b) (by association)
     joined in battle
252 *you have reason* you are right (French: *vous avez raison*)

WORTHY

If you win her you shall wear her, faith; I would not give a
fig for the conquest without the credit of the victory.

Enter KITE

KITE

Captain, Captain, a word in your ear.

PLUME

You may speak out, here are none but friends.   260

KITE

You know, sir, that you sent me to comfort the good woman
in the straw, Mrs Molly – my wife, Mr Worthy.

WORTHY

Oho! Very well – I wish you joy, Mr Kite.

KITE

Your worship very well may – for I have got both a wife and
a child in half an hour – but as I was a-saying, you sent me   265
to comfort Mrs Molly – my wife, I mean – but what d'ye
think, sir? She was better comforted before I came.

PLUME

As how?

KITE

Why, sir, a footman in a blue livery had brought her ten
guineas to buy her baby clothes.   270

PLUME

Who in the name of wonder could send them?

KITE

Nay, sir, I must whisper that – (*Whispers*) Mrs Silvia.

PLUME

Silvia! Generous creature.

WORTHY

Silvia! Impossible.

KITE

Here be the guineas, sir; I took the gold as part of my wife's 275
portion. Nay, farther, sir, she sent word the child should be
taken all imaginable care of, and that she intended to stand
godmother. The same footman, as I was coming to you with

272 s.d. *Whispers* Q2 (*Whispers* PLUME Q1)
276 *portion* dowry
     word the Q2 (word that the Q1)

257 *win . . . wear.* 'Win it and wear it' is a proverbial phrase (gain something
     and so possess it by right): Tilley W408.

this news, called after me, and told me that his lady would
speak with me – I went, and upon hearing that you were　280
come to town, she gave me half a guinea for the news, and
ordered me to tell you, that Justice Balance, her father, who
is just come out of the country, would be glad to see you.

PLUME

There's a girl for you, Worthy – is there anything of
woman in this? No, 'tis noble and generous, manly friend-　285
ship; show me another woman that would lose an inch of
her prerogative that way, without tears, fits, and reproaches.
The common jealousy of her sex, which is nothing but their
avarice of pleasure, she despises; and can part with the lover,
though she dies for the man. – Come, Worthy, where's the　290
best wine? For there I'll quarter.

WORTHY

Horton has a fresh pipe of choice Barcelona, which I would
not let him pierce before, because I reserved the maidenhead of it for your welcome to town.

PLUME

Let's away then – Mr Kite, wait on the lady with my humble　295
service, and tell her I shall only refresh a little, and wait
upon her.

WORTHY

Hold, Kite – have you seen the other recruiting captain?

KITE

No, sir.

PLUME

Another? Who is he?　　　　　　　　　　　　　　　　300

WORTHY

My rival in the first place, and the most unaccountable
fellow; but I'll tell you more as we go.　　　　　*Exeunt*

292 *pipe* winecask holding 105 imperial gallons; or, this quantity
296 *her I* Q2 (her that I Q1)
297 *upon* Q2 (on Q1)
301 *unaccountable* puzzling in behaviour

---

292 *Horton*. Dixon identifies as 'probably the Edward Haughton who was an
　　inn-keeper in Castle Ward, Shrewsbury, in 1704'; conceivably the
　　proprietor of the Maiden's Head, or Maidenhead, in the market square.
　　Barcelona. Wine from Barcelona: 'being at war with France, it was
　　considered patriotic not to drink French wine' (Ashton, p. 151); and in
　　1706 the name recalled the Allies' capture of the city in the previous
　　September.

[Act I], Scene ii

MELINDA's *Apartment*
MELINDA *and* SILVIA *meeting*

MELINDA

Welcome to town, cousin Silvia. (*Salute*) I envied you your
retreat in the country; for Shrewsbury, methinks, and all
your heads of shires, are the most irregular places for living;
here we have smoke, noise, scandal, affectation, and preten-
sion; in short, everything to give the spleen, and nothing to   5
divert it – then the air is intolerable.

SILVIA

Oh, madam, I have heard the town commended for its air.

MELINDA

But you don't consider, Silvia, how long I have lived in't!
For I can assure you, that to a lady the least nice in her
constitution, no air can be good above half a year; change of   10
air I take to be the most agreeable of any variety in life.

SILVIA

As you say, cousin Melinda, there are several sorts of airs:
airs in conversation, airs in behaviour, airs in dress; then we
have our quality airs, our sickly airs, our reserved airs, and
sometimes our impudent airs.   15

MELINDA

Psha! I talk only of the air we breathe or more properly of
that we taste – have not you, Silvia, found a vast difference in
the taste of airs?

SILVIA

Pray, cousin, are not vapours a sort of air? Taste air! You
might as well tell me I may feed on air. But prithee, my dear   20
Melinda, don't put on such an air to me; your education and
mine were just the same, and I remember the time when we
never troubled our heads about air, but when the sharp air

0.2   s.d. MELINDA's Ed. (*An* Q)
1   s.d. *Salute* kiss
3   *heads of shires* county towns
8   *in't* Q2 (in it Q1)
13–15 *airs in . . . airs* (*om.* Q2) affectations of manner
16   *Psha*! Q2 (Pshaw, Q1)
20   *might . . . may* Q2 (may . . . might Q1)
21   *an air* Q2 (airs Q1)

from the Welsh mountains made our noses drop in a cold
morning at the boarding-school.	25
MELINDA

Our education, cousin, was the same, but our temperaments
had nothing alike; you have the constitution of a horse –
SILVIA

So far as to be troubled with neither spleen, colic, nor
vapours; I need no salt for my stomach, no hartshorn for my
head, nor wash for my complexion; I can gallop all the	30
morning after the hunting-horn, and all the evening after a
fiddle. In short, I can do everything with my father but drink
and shoot flying; and I'm sure I can do everything my
mother could, were I put to the trial.
MELINDA

You're in a fair way of being put to't; for I'm told your	35
captain is come to town.
SILVIA

Aye, Melinda, he is come, and I'll take care he shan't go
without a companion.
MELINDA

You're certainly mad, cousin.
SILVIA

And there's a pleasure, sure, in being mad,	40
Which none but madmen know.
MELINDA

Thou poor, romantic Quixote, hast thou the vanity to
imagine that a young, sprightly officer that rambles o'er half
the globe in half a year, can confine his thoughts to the little
daughter of a country justice in an obscure corner of the	45
world?
SILVIA

Pshaw! What care I for his thoughts? I should not like a man
with confined thoughts, it shows a narrowness of soul.
Constancy is but a dull, sleepy quality at best, they will
hardly admit it among the manly virtues; nor do I think it	50
deserves a place with bravery, knowledge, policy, justice, and
some other qualities that are proper to that noble sex. In

24 *noses drop* Q1 (fingers ache Q2)	29 *hartshorn* smelling-salts
35 *You're* Ed. (You're are Q1; You are Q2)
43 *o'er* Q2 (over Q1)

40–1 *And . . . know.* Torrismond's comment on his apparently hopeless
love for the Queen of Arragon, in Dryden's *The Spanish Friar* (II. ii).

short, Melinda, I think a petticoat a mighty simple thing, and I'm heartily tired of my sex.

MELINDA

That is, you are tired of an appendix to our sex, that you   55
can't so handsomely get rid of in petticoats as if you were in breeches. O'my conscience, Silvia, hadst thou been a man, thou hadst been the greatest rake in Christendom.

SILVIA

I should endeavour to know the world, which a man can never do thoroughly without half a hundred friendships, and   60
as many amours. But now I think on't, how stands your affair with Mr Worthy?

MELINDA

He's my aversion.

SILVIA

Vapours!

MELINDA

What do you say, madam?   65

SILVIA

I say that you should not use that honest fellow so in-humanely. He's a gentleman of parts and fortune, and beside that he's my Plume's friend, and by all that's sacred, if you don't use him better, I shall expect satisfaction.

MELINDA

Satisfaction! You begin to fancy yourself in breeches in good   70
earnest. But to be plain with you, I like Worthy the worse for being so intimate with your captain, for I take him to be a loose, idle, unmannerly coxcomb.

SILVIA

Oh, madam! You never saw him, perhaps, since you were mistress of twenty thousand pound; you only knew him when   75
you were capitulating with Worthy for a settlement, which perhaps might encourage him to be a little loose and un-mannerly with you.

MELINDA

What do you mean, madam?

SILVIA

My meaning needs no interpretation, madam.   80

MELINDA

Better it had, madam, for methinks you're too plain.

55 *appendix* appendage, i.e., modesty, virginity
64 *Vapours!* (Vapours. Q1) 'mere affectation' ex. (a) something
    insubstantial; (b) modish hypochondria (Dixon)
69 *expect satisfaction* i.e., challenge you to a duel

SILVIA

　If you mean the plainness of my person, I think your ladyship as plain as me to the full.

MELINDA

　Were I assured of that, I should be glad to take up with a
rakehelly officer as you do.　　85

SILVIA

　Again! Look'ee, madam – you're in your own house.

MELINDA

　And if you had kept in yours, I should have excused you.

SILVIA

　Don't be troubled, madam, I shan't desire to have my visit
returned.

MELINDA

　The sooner therefore you make an end of this the better.　　90

SILVIA

　I'm easily advised to follow my inclinations – so, madam –
your humble servant.　　　　　　　　　　　　　　　　*Exit*

MELINDA

　Saucy thing!

Enter LUCY

LUCY

　What's the matter, madam?

MELINDA

　Did you not see the proud nothing, how she swells upon the　　95
arrival of her fellow?

LUCY

　Her fellow has not been long enough arrived to occasion any
great swelling, madam; I don't believe she has seen him yet.

MELINDA

　Nor shan't if I can help it; let me see – I have it – bring me
pen and ink – hold, I'll go write in my closet.　　100

LUCY

　An answer to this letter, I hope, madam.　(*Presents a letter*)

MELINDA

　Who sent it?

LUCY

　Your captain, madam.

MELINDA

　He's a fool, and I'm tired of him, send it back unopened.

LUCY

　The messenger's gone, madam.　　105

　85 *rakehelly* Q2 (rakely Q1)

MELINDA

Then how shall I send an answer? Call him back immediately, while I go write.   *Exeunt*

Act II, Scene i

An Apartment [in JUSTICE BALANCE's *House]*
Enter JUSTICE BALANCE *and* PLUME

BALANCE

Look'ee, Captain, give us but blood for our money, and you
shan't want men. I remember that for some years of the last
war we had no blood nor wounds but in the officers' mouths,
nothing for our millions but newspapers not worth a reading
– our armies did nothing but play at prison bars and hide-   5
and-seek with the enemy; but now ye have brought us
colours and standards and prisoners; odsmylife, Captain, get
us but another Marshal of France, and I'll go myself for a
soldier.

PLUME

Pray, Mr Balance, how does your fair daughter?   10

BALANCE

Ah, Captain, what is my daughter to a Marshal of France?
We're upon a nobler subject. I want to have a particular
description of the Battle of Höchstädt.

107 s.d. *Exeunt* Q2 (*Exeunt severally* Q1)
  8, 11 •*Marshal* Q2 (Mareschal Q1)

2–3 *the last war*. The War of the League of Augsburg (1689–97) 'had been
  sluggish and unexciting' (Archer), made up chiefly of manoeuvring and
  minor sieges, apart from the capture of Marshal Boufflers at Namur in
  1695. The levels of new taxes (e.g., land tax at 4 shillings in the pound)
  to pay for the wars, aroused great resentment; but this was eased in the
  national satisfaction over Marlborough's brilliant victories.
5 *prison bars*. West Country tag game, in which a 'keeper' tried to 'imprison'
  pairs of players behind a stump or stone (Dixon).
7–8 *colours . . . France*. Marlborough's trophies and prisoners captured at
  Blenheim, including Marshal Tallard and sixteen generals. They were
  brought to London and paraded, amid great public rejoicing, on
  5 January 1705. Tallard spent the next few years in Nottingham, and
  became a well-known, popular figure.
13 *the Battle of Höchstädt*. i.e., Blenheim, fought on 13 August 1704. The
  Franco-Bavarian forces occupied the villages of Lutzingen and Blenheim, and the ground between them, east of Höchstädt. Here they were
  attacked by the Grand Alliance army under Marlborough and Prince
  Eugene.

PLUME

The battle, sir, was a very pretty battle as one should desire to
see, but we were all so intent upon victory that we never   15
minded the battle; all that I know of the matter is, our
general commanded us to beat the French, and we did so,
and if he pleases to say the word, we'll do't again. – But pray,
sir, how does Mrs Silvia?

BALANCE

Still upon Silvia! For shame, Captain – you're engaged   20
already, wedded to the war; victory is your mistress, and it
is below a soldier to think of any other.

PLUME

As a mistress, I confess, but as a friend, Mr Balance.

BALANCE

Come, come, Captain, never mince the matter, would not
you debauch my daughter if you could?   25

PLUME

How, sir! I hope she's not to be debauched.

BALANCE

Faith, but she is, sir, and any woman in England of her age
and complexion, by a man of your youth and vigour. Look'ee,
Captain, once I was young and once an officer as you are, and
I can guess at your thoughts now by what mine were then,   30
and I remember very well, that I would have given one of my
legs to have deluded the daughter of an old, plain country
gentleman, as like me as I was then like you.

PLUME

But, sir, was that country gentleman your friend and
benefactor?   35

BALANCE

Not much of that.

PLUME

There the comparison breaks; the favours, sir, that –

BALANCE

Pho, I hate speeches. If I have done you any service, Captain,
'twas to please myself, for I love thee; and if I could part with
my girl, you should have her as soon as any young fellow I   40
know; I hope you have more honour than to quit the service,

17 *general* Q2 (generals Q1) Marlborough   21 *victory* Q2 (war Q1)
26 *she's* Q2 (she is Q1)   41 *know; I* Q2 (know; but I Q1)

---

18 *and if . . again.* Not mere rhetoric, but a reflection of the full, and
justified, confidence his army had in him (see A. L. Rowse, *The Early
Churchills* [Harmondsworth, 1959], p. 294).

and she more prudence than to follow the camp. But she's
at her own disposal, she has fifteen hundred pound in her
pocket, and so – Silvia, Silvia!   *Calls*

Enter SILVIA

SILVIA

There are some letters, sir, come by the post from London;   45
I left them upon the table in your closet.

BALANCE

And here is a gentleman from Germany. (*Presents* PLUME *to
her*) Captain, you'll excuse me, I'll go read my letters, and
wait on you.   *Exit*

SILVIA

Sir, you're welcome to England.   50

PLUME

You are indebted to me a welcome, madam, since the hopes
of receiving it from this fair hand was the principal cause of
my seeing England.

SILVIA

I have often heard that soldiers were sincere, shall I venture
to believe public report?   55

PLUME

You may, when 'tis backed by private insurance; for I
swear, madam, by the honour of my profession, that whatever dangers I went upon, it was with the hope of making
myself more worthy of your esteem, and if I ever had
thoughts of preserving my life, 'twas for the pleasure of   60
dying at your feet.

SILVIA

Well, well, you shall die at my feet, or where you will; but
you know, sir, there is a certain will and testament to be made
beforehand.

PLUME

My will, madam, is made already, and there it is. (*Gives her*   65
a parchment) And if you please to open that parchment,
which was drawn the evening before the Battle of Blenheim,
you will find whom I left my heir.

SILVIA *opens the will and reads*

51–64 So Q2 (Q1, see Appendix 1, A, i)
56 *insurance* (a) assurance; (b) in the modern sense

59–61 The equivoque on 'die' ('experience sexual orgasm') links this
    declaration to their dispute about marriage and consummation; see
    I.i, 229–34.

SILVIA

'Mrs Silvia Balance'. – Well, Captain, this is a handsome
and a substantial compliment; but I can assure you I am   70
much better pleased with the bare knowledge of your
intention than I should have been in the possession of your
legacy; but methinks, sir, you should have left something to
your little boy at the Castle.

PLUME

(*Aside*) That's home. – My little boy! Lack-a-day, madam,   75
that alone may convince you 'twas none of mine; why the
girl, madam, is my sergeant's wife, and so the poor creature
gave out that I was father in hopes that my friends might
support her in case of necessity; that was all, madam. – My
boy! No, no, no.   80

Enter SERVANT

SERVANT

Madam, my master has received some ill news from London
and desires to speak with you immediately, and he begs the
captain's pardon that he can't wait on him as he promised.

PLUME

Ill news! Heavens avert it; nothing could touch me nearer
than to see that generous, worthy gentleman afflicted; I'll 85
leave you to comfort him, and be assured that if my life and
fortune can be any way serviceable to the father of my Silvia,
he shall freely command both.

SILVIA

The necessity must be very pressing that would engage me
to endanger either.   *Exeunt severally*   90

[Act II], Scene ii

Another Apartment
Enter BALANCE *and* SILVIA

SILVIA

Whilst there is life there is hope, sir; perhaps my brother may
recover.

80 *No, no, no* Q2 (No, no Q1)
88 *he* Q2 (she Q1)
90 *endanger* Q2 (do Q1)
   0.2 s.d. *Another Apartment* Ed. (SCENE *changes to another Apartment*
        Q1; SCENE, *Another Apartment* Q2)
   1 *Whilst . . . hope* proverbial. Tilley, L 269

BALANCE

We have but little reason to expect it. Dr Kilman acquaints
me here, that before this comes to my hands he fears I shall
have no son. – Poor Owen! But the decree is just; I was   5
pleased with the death of my father, because he left me an
estate, and now I'm punished with the loss of an heir to
inherit mine. I must now look upon you as the only hopes of
my family, and I expect that the augmentation of your
fortune will give you fresh thoughts and new prospects.   10

SILVIA

My desire of being punctual in my obedience requires that
you would be plain in your commands, sir.

BALANCE

The death of your brother makes you sole heiress to my
estate, which you know is about twelve hundred pounds a
year; this fortune gives you a fair claim to quality and a title;   15
you must set a just value upon yourself, and in plain terms
think no more of Captain Plume.

SILVIA

You have often commended the gentleman, sir.

BALANCE

And I do so still; he's a very pretty fellow; but though I
liked him well enough for a bare son-in-law, I don't approve   20
of him for an heir to my estate and family; fifteen hundred
pound, indeed, I might trust in his hands, and it might do
the young fellow a kindness, but odsmylife, twelve hundred
pound a year would ruin him, quite turn his brain. A
captain of foot worth twelve hundred pound a year! 'Tis a   25
prodigy in nature. Besides this, I have five or six thousand
pounds in woods upon my estate; oh, that would make him
stark mad! For you must know that all captains have a
mighty aversion to timber, they can't endure to see trees

11 *punctual* punctilious
14–15 *which you . . . year* Q2 (which three or four years hence will
    amount to twelve hundred pound *per annum* Q1)
15 *fair . . . title* i.e., to marry a man with both
23 *odsmylife* mild oath, from 'God save my life'

24–6 *A captain . . . nature.* A captain of foot received about £100 a year
    (see Stonehill, II, 434).

standing. Then I should have some rogue of a builder by the　30
help of his damned magic art transform my noble oaks and
elms into cornishes, portals, sashes, birds, beasts, gods, and
devils, to adorn some maggoty, new-fashioned bauble under
the Thames; and then you should have a dog of a gardener
bring a *habeas corpus* for my *terra firma*, remove it to Chelsea　35
or Twit'nam, and clap it into grass-plats and gravel walks.

Enter a SERVANT

SERVANT
Sir, here's one below with a letter for your worship, but he
will deliver it into no hands but your own.
BALANCE
Come, show me the messenger.　　　　　*Exit with* SERVANT
SILVIA
Make the dispute between love and duty, and I am Prince　40
Prettyman exactly. – If my brother dies, ah, poor brother!
If he lives, ah, poor sister! – 'Tis bad both ways; I'll try it
again, – follow my own inclinations and break my father's
heart, or obey his commands and break my own; worse and
worse. Suppose I take it thus – a moderate fortune, a pretty　45
fellow, and a pad; or a fine estate, a coach-and-six, and an
ass – that will never do neither.

Enter BALANCE *and* SERVANT

BALANCE
Put four horses into the coach.
　　　　　　　　　　　　To the SERVANT, *who goes out*
Ho, Silvia –
SILVIA
Sir.　　　　　　　　　　　　　　　　　　　　　　　　50

32 *cornishes* cornices
35 *habeas corpus* literally, writ requiring that a person be brought
　before a judge or into court
36 *Twit'nam* Twickenham　　　　*grass-plats* lawns
42 *try it* Q2 (try Q1)　　　49 *Ho,* Q2 (not in Q1)

30–6 *Then . . . walks.* Many of the nobility and gentry were moving to
　London during this decade, building houses in the western quarter.
　Chelsea and Twickenham were then small-town areas to the west. (See
　John Loftis, *Comedy and Society from Congreve to Fielding* [Stanford,
　1959], pp. 12–13).
40–1 *Prince Prettyman.* In Buckingham's *The Rehearsal* (III.ii), where it is
　Volscius who is pulled between the claims of love and honour. Farquhar
　makes the same error in *Love and Business* (Stonehill, II, 305, 434).

BALANCE

How old were you when your mother died?

SILVIA

So young that I don't remember I ever had one; and you have been so careful, so indulgent to me since, that indeed I never wanted one.

BALANCE

Have I ever denied you anything you asked of me? 55

SILVIA

Never, that I remember.

BALANCE

Then, Silvia, I must beg that once in your life you would grant me a favour.

SILVIA

Why should you question it, sir?

BALANCE

I don't, but I would rather counsel than command; I don't 60 propose this with the authority of a parent, but as the advice of your friend, that you would take the coach this moment and go into the country.

SILVIA

Does this advice, sir, proceed from the contents of the letter you received just now? 65

BALANCE

No matter; I will be with you in three or four days and then give you my reasons. But before you go, I expect you will make me one solemn promise.

SILVIA

Propose the thing, sir.

BALANCE

That you will never dispose of yourself to any man without 70 my consent.

SILVIA

I promise.

BALANCE

Very well, and to be even with you, I promise that I will never dispose of you without your own consent; and so, Silvia, the coach is ready; farewell. (*Leads her to the door and returns*) 75 Now she's gone, I'll examine the contents of this letter a little nearer. (*Reads*)

    Sir,

        My intimacy with Mr Worthy has drawn a secret from

64 *sir,* Q2 (not in Q1)   66 *will* Q2 (shall Q1)

him that he had from his friend Captain Plume, and my   80
friendship and relation to your family oblige me to give
you timely notice of it: the captain has dishonourable
designs upon my cousin Silvia. Evils of this nature are
more easily prevented than amended, and that you would
immediately send my cousin into the country is the advice   85
of,

Sir, your humble servant,
MELINDA.

Why, the devil's in the young fellows of this age; they're ten
times worse than they were in my time! Had he made my   90
daughter a whore and forswore it like a gentleman, I could
have almost pardoned it; but to tell tales beforehand is
monstrous! Hang it, I can fetch down a woodcock or snipe,
and why not a hat and feather? I have a case of good pistols,
and have a good mind to try.   95

Enter WORTHY

BALANCE

Worthy, your servant.

WORTHY

I'm sorry, sir, to be the messenger of ill news.

BALANCE

I apprehend it, sir; you have heard that my son Owen is past
recovery.

WORTHY

My advices say he's dead, sir.   100

BALANCE

He's happy, and I am satisfied; the strokes of heaven I can
bear; but injuries from men, Mr Worthy, are not so easily
supported.

WORTHY

I hope, sir, you're under no apprehension of wrong from
anybody?   105

BALANCE

You know I ought to be.

WORTHY

You wrong my honour, sir, in believing I could know anything to your prejudice without resenting it as much as you
should.

BALANCE

This letter, sir, which I tear in pieces to conceal the person   110

100 *advices* news from afar   104 *you're* Q2 (you are Q1)

that sent it, informs me that Plume has a design upon Silvia,
and that you are privy to't.

WORTHY

Nay then, sir, I must do myself justice and endeavour to find
out the author. (*Takes up a bit*) Sir, I know the hand, and if
you refuse to discover the contents, Melinda shall tell me.   115
Going

BALANCE

Hold, sir, the contents I have told you already, only with this
circumstance, that her intimacy with Mr Worthy had drawn
the secret from him.

WORTHY

Her intimacy with me! – Dear sir, let me pick up the pieces
of this letter; 'twill give me such a hank upon her pride, to   120
have her own an intimacy under her hand; 'twas the luckiest
accident. (*Gathering up the letter*) The aspersion, sir, was
nothing but malice, the effect of a little quarrel between her
and Mrs Silvia.

BALANCE

Are you sure of that, sir?   125

WORTHY

Her maid gave me the history of part of the battle just now,
as she overheard it.

BALANCE

'Tis probable, I am satisfied.

WORTHY

But I hope, sir, your daughter has suffered nothing upon the
account?   130

BALANCE

No, no – poor girl, she's so afflicted with the news of her
brother's death that to avoid company she begged leave to
be gone into the country.

WORTHY

And is she gone?

BALANCE

I could not refuse her, she was so pressing; the coach went   135
from the door the minute before you came.

WORTHY

So pressing to be gone, sir! – I find her fortune will give her
the same airs with Melinda, and then Plume and I may
laugh at one another.

114 s.d. *bit* Q2 (*piece of the letter* Q1)   120 *hank* hold
128 so, Q1 (speech omitted Q2)
131 *she's* Q2 (she is Q1)

BALANCE

    Like enough; women are as subject to pride as we are, and 140
why mayn't great women as well as great men forget their old
acquaintance? But come, where's this young fellow? I love
him so well it would break the heart of me to think him a
rascal. – (*Aside*) I'm glad my daughter's gone fairly off
though. – Where does the captain quarter? 145

WORTHY

    At Horton's; I'm to meet him there two hours hence, and we
should be glad of your company.

BALANCE

    Your pardon, dear Worthy, I must allow a day or two to the
death of my son; the decorum of mourning is what we owe
the world because they pay it to us. Afterwards, I'm yours 150
over a bottle, or how you will.

WORTHY

    Sir, I'm your humble servant.   *Exeunt severally*

[Act II], Scene iii

The Street

Enter KITE, [*leading* COSTAR PEARMAIN *in one hand, and* THOMAS
APPLETREE *in the other, both drunk*]

KITE (*Sings*)

        Our prentice Tom may now refuse
        To wipe his scoundrel master's shoes,
        For now he's free to sing and play,
        Over the hills and far away.
           Over, &c.   5
      [APPLETREE *and* PEARMAIN *join in the chorus*]

150 *us. Afterwards, I'm* Ed. (us afterwards. I'm Q)
  0.1–0.2 s.d. *leading . . . drunk* Ed. (*with one of the Mob in each hand,
    drunk* Q1)
  1 KITE (*Sings*) Ed. (0.1 Kite *sings* Q)
  5, 10 *Over,&c* Q2 (*Over the hills,* &c Q1)
  5 s.d. APPLETREE . . . *chorus* Ed. (*The Mob sing the Chorus* Q)

  0.1, s.d. etc. COSTAR PEARMAIN . . . THOMAS APPLETREE. Farquhar's '1st
    Mob' and '2d Mob' give their names in full at the end of the scene, and
    are identified by name in later C18 editions. The speech prefixes in
    Q1–4 are confused: before Plume's entry at l.46, '1st Mob' is clearly
    Thomas, and after it he is addressed as Costar; similarly '2d Mob' is
    Costar initially and then Thomas.
  1–10 Verses 10 and 12 of 'The Recruiting Officer'; see Appendix 2. The
    chorus is as sung by Plume, ll. 48–51 below.

> We all shall lead more happy lives,
> By getting rid of brats and wives,
> That scold and brawl both night and day,
> Over the hills and far away.
>> Over, &c.   10

Hey, boys! Thus we soldiers live; drink, sing, dance, play;
we live, as one should say – we live – 'tis impossible to tell
how we live. We're all princes – why – why, you're a king –
you're an emperor, and I'm a prince – now – an't we? –

APPLETREE

No, Sergeant – I'll be no emperor.   15

KITE

No?

APPLETREE

No, I'll be a justice of peace.

KITE

A justice of peace, man!

APPLETREE

Aye, wauns will I, for since this Pressing Act they are greater
than any emperor under the sun.   20

KITE

Done; you're a justice of peace, and you're a king, and I'm a
duke, and a rum duke, an't I?

PEARMAIN

No, but I'll be no king.

KITE

What then?

PEARMAIN

I'll be a queen.   25

KITE

A queen!

PEARMAIN

Aye, Queen of England, that's greater than any king of 'em
all.

KITE

Bravely said, faith! Huzza for the Queen!   *All huzza*

15, etc. s.p. APPLETREE Ed. (1st *Mob* Q)
22 *rum* excellent (O.E.D.,a¹); *rum duke* showily handsome man
23, etc. s.p. PEARMAIN Ed. (2nd *Mob* Q1)

---

19 *this Pressing Act.* The Impressment Act of 1703, 2° and 3° Anne, cap.
   xiii, and others in 1704 and 1705, empowered three justices to impress
   any man who lacked lawful employment or means of support.

But hark'ee you Mr Justice and you Mr Queen, did you ever   30
see the Queen's picture?

BOTH

No, no, no.

KITE

I wonder at that; I have two of 'em set in gold, and as like
Her Majesty, God bless the mark. (*He takes two broad pieces
out of his pocket*) See here, they're set in gold.   35
                                              Gives one to each

APPLETREE

The wonderful works of Nature!   *Looking at it*

PEARMAIN

What's this written about? Here's a posy, I believe, *Ca-ro-lus*
– what's that, Sergeant?

KITE

Oh, *Carolus*! Why, *Carolus* is Latin for Queen Anne, that's
all.   40

PEARMAIN

'Tis a fine thing to be a scollard – Sergeant, will you part
with this? I'll buy it on you, if it come within the compass of
a crawn.

KITE

A crown! Never talk of buying; 'tis the same thing among
friends, you know, I present 'em to you both; you shall give   45
me as good a thing. Put 'em up, and remember your old
friend, when I'm *over the hills and far away*.   *Singing*
                                       They sing and put up the money

32 *No, no, no* Q2 (No, no Q1)
34 *God bless the mark* exclamation by way of apology, for taking her
   name in vain
36 s.d. *Looking at it* Q2 (*Looking earnestly upon the piece* Q1)
37 *posy* short motto, usually in verse
45, 46, 62, 97 *'em* Q2 (them Q1)

34 s.d. *broad pieces*. Gold coins, originally valued at 20*s.*; here, doubtless,
   hammered unites struck between 1660 and 1662, on which the king's
   bust could plausibly be passed off as 'the Queen's picture', unlike that of
   the bearded Charles I. The bust of Charles II appears on the obverse,
   'in profile to the left, laureate, with long hair, neck bare, and armour
   with a scarf over it', together with the legend 'CAROLVS. II. D.G. MAG.
   BRIT. FRAN. ET. HIB. REX.', and, initially, no value-designation (Sir
   Geoffrey Duveen and H. G. Stride, *The History of the Gold Sovereign*
   [London, 1962], pp. 44–8, plate 10c).
47 s.d. N.T. 'Plume's entry is not fortuitous: he enters at a signal from
   Kite' (Tynan).

Enter PLUME *singing*

PLUME

> Over the hills, and o're the main,
> To Flanders, Portugal, or Spain;
> The Queen commands, and we'll obey,   50
> Over the hills and far away.

Come on my men of mirth, away with it, I'll make one
among ye. – Who are these hearty lads?

KITE

Off with your hats; ouns, off with your hats; this is the
captain, the captain.   55

APPLETREE

We have seen captains afore now, mun.

PEARMAIN

Aye, and lieutenant captains too; flesh, I'se keep on my nab.

APPLETREE

And I'se scarcely d'off mine for any captain in England; my
vether's a freeholder.

PLUME

Who are these jolly lads, Sergeant?   60

KITE

A couple of honest, brave fellows that are willing to serve the
Queen; I have entertained 'em just now as volunteers under
your honour's command.

PLUME

And good entertainment they shall have; volunteers are the
men I want, those are the men fit to make soldiers, captains,   65
generals.

PEARMAIN

Wauns, Tummas, what's this? Are you listed?

APPLETREE

Flesh, not I; are you, Costar?

PEARMAIN

Wauns, not I.

KITE

What, not listed! Ha, ha, ha, a very good jest, faith.   70

PEARMAIN

Come, Tummas, we'll go whome.

APPLETREE

Aye, aye, come.

51 *hills* Q2 (hill Q1)
57 *nab* hat
67 *listed* i.e., enlisted

KITE

Home! For shame, gentlemen, behave yourselves better
before your captain – dear Tummas, honest Costar –

PEARMAIN

No, no, we'll be gone.   *Going*   75

KITE

Nay, then I command you to stay: I place you both sentinels
in this place for two hours to watch the motion of St Mary's
clock, you, and you the motion of St Chad's; and he that dare
stir from his post till he be relieved shall have my sword in
his guts the next minute.   80

PLUME

What's the matter, Sergeant? I'm afraid you're too rough
with these gentlemen.

KITE

I'm too mild, sir, they disobey command, sir, and one of 'em
should be shot for an example to the other.

PEARMAIN

Shot, Tummas!   85

PLUME

Come, gentlemen, what's the matter?

APPLETREE

We don't know; the noble sergeant is pleased to be in a
passion, sir – but –

KITE

They disobey command, they deny their being listed.

PEARMAIN

Nay, Sergeant, we don't downright deny it neither, that we   90
dare not do for fear of being shot; but we humbly conceive
in a civil way, and begging your worship's pardon, that we
may go home.

---

86 *what's* Q2 (what is Q1)

77–8 *St Mary's . . . St Chad's* St Mary's Church, founded in the C10, and
      containing much Norman work, remains intact. It 'has a chiming clock
      with . . . four bells' (Jeffares). The old St Chad's, also founded in Saxon
      times, was roughly south-west of St Mary's. It collapsed in 1788,
      leaving only the lady-chapel standing, and the new St Chad's was built
      in 1790–92 farther westward.
83–4 *one . . . other.* N.T.: 'During rehearsals Kite improvised as follows:
      ". . . and they both should be shot as an example to one another." This
      impromptu—a distinct improvement on Farquhar's original—was
      retained in performance' (Tynan).

PLUME

 That's easily known; have either of you received any of the
 Queen's money?   95

APPLETREE

 Not a brass farthing, sir.

KITE

 Sir, they have each of 'em received three and twenty shillings
 and sixpence, and 'tis now in their pockets.

APPLETREE

 Wauns! If I have a penny in my pocket but a bent sixpence,
 I'll be content to be listed, and shot into the bargain. 100

PEARMAIN

 And I, look'ee here, sir.

APPLETREE

 Aye, here's my stock too, nothing but the Queen's picture
 that the sergeant gave me just now.

KITE

 See there, a broad piece, three and twenty shillings and
 sixpence; the t'other has the fellow on't.   105

PLUME

 The case is plain, gentlemen, the goods are found upon you:
 those pieces of gold are worth three and twenty and sixpence
 each.

PEARMAIN

 So it seems that *Carolus* is three and twenty shillings and
 sixpence in Latin.   110

APPLETREE

 'Tis the same thing in the Greek, for we are listed.

PEARMAIN

 Flesh, but we an't, Tummas; I desire to be carried before
 the mayar, Captain.
     While they talk, the CAPTAIN *and* SERGEANT *whisper*

PLUME

 'Twill never do, Kite; your damned tricks will ruin me at last
 – I won't lose the fellows though, if I can help it. – Well, 115
 gentlemen, there must be some trick in this; my sergeant
 offers to take his oath that you're fairly listed.

APPLETREE

 Why, Captain, we know that you soldiers have more liberty
 of conscience than other folks, but for me or neighbour
 Costar here to take such an oath, 'twould be downright 120
 perjuration.

102 *stock* total property
117 *offers to* Q2 (offers here to Q1)

PLUME

Look'ee you rascal, you villain, if I find that you have imposed upon these two honest fellows, I'll trample you to death, you dog; come, how was't?

APPLETREE

Nay, then we will speak. Your sergeant, as you say, is a rogue, 125 begging your worship's pardon, and –

PEARMAIN

Nay, Tummas, let me speak, you know I can read. – And so, sir, he gave us those two pieces of money for pictures of the Queen by way of a present.

PLUME

How! By way of a present! The son of a whore! I'll teach 130 him to abuse honest fellows like you. Scoundrel, rogue, villain, *etc.*   *Beats off the* SERGEANT, *and follows*

BOTH

O brave, noble Captain! Huzza! A brave captain, faith.

PEARMAIN

Now, Tummas, *Carolus* is Latin for a beating; this is the bravest captain I ever saw. – Wauns, I have a month's mind 135 to go with him.

Enter PLUME

PLUME

A dog, to abuse two such honest fellows as you! Look'ee, gentlemen, I love a pretty fellow; I come among you here as an officer to list soldiers, not as a kidnapper to steal slaves.

PEARMAIN

Mind that, Tummas.   140

PLUME

I desire no man to go with me, but as I went myself: I went a volunteer, as you or you may go, for a little time carried a musket, and now I command a company.

APPLETREE

Mind that, Costar, a sweet gentleman.

---

132 s.d. *Beats . . . follows* Q2 (*Beats the Serjeant off the stage, and follows him out* Q1)
135 *a month's mind* an inclination (proverbial phrase: Tilley M1109)
136 s.d. *Enter* Q2 (*Re-enter* Q1)
137 *honest* Q2 (pretty Q1)

---

132 *villain, etc.* An invitation to improvise, to which contemporary actors were deplorably prone (see Nicoll, pp. 41–2).

PLUME

    'Tis true, gentlemen, I might take an advantage of you; the   145
Queen's money was in your pockets, my sergeant was ready
to take his oath you were listed; but I scorn to do a base thing,
you are both of you at your liberty.

PEARMAIN

    Thank you, noble Captain. – I cod, I can't find in my heart
to leave him, he talks so finely.   150

APPLETREE

    Aye, Costar, would he always hold in this mind.

PLUME

    Come, my lads, one thing more I'll tell you: you're both
young, tight fellows, and the army is the place to make you
men forever: every man has his lot, and you have yours.
What think you now of a purse full of French gold out of a   155
monsieur's pocket, after you have dashed out his brains with
the butt of your firelock, eh?

PEARMAIN

    Wauns, I'll have it, Captain – give me a shilling, I'll follow
you to the end of the world.

APPLETREE

    Nay, dear Costar, duna; be advised.   160

PLUME

    Here, my hero, here are two guineas for thee, as earnest of
what I'll do farther for thee.

APPLETREE

    Duna take it, duna, dear Costar.

                             (*Cries, and pulls back his arm*)

PEARMAIN

    I wull, I wull – wauns, my mind gives me that I shall be a
captain myself. I take your money, sir, and now I'm a   165
gentleman.

PLUME

    Give me thy hand. – And now you and I will travel the world
o'er, and command wherever we tread. – [*Aside to*
PEARMAIN] Bring your friend with you if you can.

PEARMAIN

    Well, Tummas, must we part?   170

---

147 *oath you* Q2 (oath that you Q1)
149 *I cod* softened oath, cognate with 'egad'
    can't Q2 (cannot Q1)
151 *always* Q2 (alway Q1)
161 *earnest* instalment of money, pledge

APPLETREE
No, Costar, I cannot leave thee. Come, Captain (*crying*), I'll
e'en go along too, and if you have two honester, simpler lads
in your company than we twa been – I'll say no more.

PLUME
Here, my lad. (*Gives him money*) Now your name?

APPLETREE
Thummas Appletree.   175

PLUME
And yours?

PEARMAIN
Costar Pearmain.

PLUME
Born where?

APPLETREE
Both in Herefordshire.

PLUME
Very well. Courage, my lads, now we'll sing *Over the hills*   180
and far away.

        Courage, boys, 'tis one to ten,
        But we return all gentlemen;
        [While conquering colours we display,
        Over the hills and far away.   185
        Over,] &c.   *Exeunt*

Act III, Scene i

The Market-place
Enter PLUME *and* WORTHY

WORTHY
I can't forbear admiring the equality of our two fortunes: we
loved two ladies, they met us halfway, and just as we were
upon the point of leaping into their arms, fortune drops into

173 *than* Q2 (that Q1)
180 *we'll* Q2 (we will Q1)
184–6 *While . . . &c.* Ed. (not in Q)
186 s.d. *Exeunt* Q2 (not in Q1)
  0.1 *Enter* Q2 (not in Q1)
  1 *can't* Ed. (can'nt Q1)

184–6 *While . . . &c.* Supplied in later C18 editions, as an alternative to
    'All gentlemen as well as they . . .' in the final verse; see Appendix 2.
    Extended endings to this scene in later C18 editions are outlined in
    Appendix 1.

their laps, pride possesses their hearts, a maggot fills their
heads, madness takes 'em by the tails, they snort, kick up their   5
heels, and away they run.

PLUME

And leave us here to mourn upon the shore – a couple of
poor, melancholy monsters – what shall we do?

WORTHY

I have a trick for mine; the letter, you know, and the fortune-
teller.   10

PLUME

And I have a trick for mine.

WORTHY

What is't?

PLUME

I'll never think of her again.

WORTHY

No!

PLUME

No; I think myself above administering to the pride of any   15
woman, were she worth twelve thousand a year, and I han't
the vanity to believe I shall ever gain a lady worth twelve
hundred; the generous, good-natured Silvia in her smock I
admire, but the haughty, scornful Silvia, with her fortune,
I despise.   20

A SONG

1

Come, fair one, be kind,
You never shall find
A fellow so fit for a lover;
The world shall view
My passion for you,   25
But never your passion discover.

4 *maggot* whim
18 *in her smock* as an unaffected, natural country girl

7–8 *And . . . monsters* Probably alluding to Caliban and his sister Sycorax
('Two Monsters of the Isle') in Davenant and Dryden's adaptation of
The Tempest, who will be left behind when the other characters sail
away. Sycorax has become Mrs Trinculo.
21–38 This song was omitted in Q2, possibly because it existed separately
from the playhouse manuscript (Kenny, II, 25–6). Richard Leveridge's
setting is given in Appendix 2, with adapted lyrics.

2

I still will complain
Of your frowns and disdain,
Though I revel through all your charms;
The world shall declare,   30
That I die with despair,
When I only die in your arms.

3

I still will adore,
And love more and more,
But, by Jove, if you chance to prove cruel: 35
I'll get me a miss
That freely will kiss,
Though I afterwards drink water-gruel.

What, sneak out o'town and not so much as a word, a line, a
compliment – 'sdeath! How far off does she live? I'll go and   40
break her windows.

WORTHY
Ha, ha, ha; aye, and the window bars too to come at her.
Come, come, friend, no more of your rough, military airs.

Enter KITE

KITE
Captain, sir, look yonder, she's a-coming this way, 'tis the
prettiest, cleanest, little tit.   45

PLUME
Now, Worthy, to show you how much I'm in love – here she
comes, and what is that great country fellow with her?

KITE
I can't tell, sir.

Enter ROSE *and her brother* BULLOCK, ROSE *with a basket on her
arm, crying* 'Chickens'

---

32 *die* experience orgasm   38 *water-gruel* fig., type of insipidness
40 *I'll* Q2 (I'd Q1)   45 *tit* small horse; fig., young woman

---

41 *break her windows.* 'This was frequently done to whores, particularly
   when the angry party had a grudge' (Stonehill, II, 435; cf. *The Twin
   Rivals*, I.i, 27).
42 *window . . . her.* Cf. Lancelot in Malory's *Mort d'Arthur*, Book 19,
   chapter 6, who entered Guinevere's bed chamber by this method.

ROSE
Buy chickens, young and tender, young and tender chickens.
PLUME
Here, you chickens!   50
ROSE
Who calls?
PLUME
Come hither, pretty maid.
ROSE
Will you please to buy, sir?
WORTHY
Yes, child, we'll both buy.
PLUME
Nay, Worthy, that's not fair, market for yourself; come,   55
child, I'll buy all you have.
ROSE
Then all I have is at your sarvice.   *Curtsies*
WORTHY
Then I must shift for myself, I find.   *Exit*
PLUME
Let me see – young and tender, you say?

                              Chucks her under the chin
ROSE
As ever you tasted in your life, sir.   *Curtsies*   60
PLUME
Come, I must examine your basket to the bottom, my dear.
ROSE
Nay, for that matter, put in your hand; feel, sir; I warrant
my ware as good as any in the market.
PLUME
And I'll buy it all, child, were it ten times more.
ROSE
Sir, I can furnish you.   65
PLUME
Come then; we won't quarrel about the price, they're fine
birds; pray what's your name, pretty creature?
ROSE
Rose, sir; my father is a farmer within three short mile o'th'
town; we keep this market; I sell chickens, eggs, and butter,
and my brother Bullock there sells corn.   70
BULLOCK
Come, sister, haste ye; we shall be liate a whome.

56 *child* Q2 (my child Q1)

All this while BULLOCK *whistles about the stage*

PLUME

Kite! (*Tips him the wink, he returns it*) Pretty Mrs Rose – you
have – let me see – how many?

ROSE

A dozen, sir, and they are richly worth a crawn.

BULLOCK

Come, Ruose, Ruose, I sold fifty stracke o'barley today in   75
half this time; but you will higgle and higgle for a penny
more than the commodity is worth.

ROSE

What's that to you, oaf? I can make as much out of a groat
as you can out of fourpence, I'm sure – the gentleman bids
fair, and when I meet with a chapman, I know how to make   80
the best on him – and so, sir, I say for a crawn piece the
bargain's yours.

PLUME

Here's a guinea, my dear.

ROSE

I con't change your money, sir.

PLUME

Indeed, indeed but you can – my lodging is hard by, chicken,   85
and we'll make change there.   *Goes off, she follows him*

KITE

So, sir, as I was telling you, I have seen one of these hussars
eat up a ravelin for his breakfast and afterwards pick his teeth
with a palisado.

BULLOCK

Aye, you soldiers see very strange things – but pray, sir,   90
what is a ravelin?

72 s.d. *Tips . . . it* Q2 (*He tips the wink upon* Kite, *who returns it* Q1)
75 *stracke* (strake Q2) strike(s), usually identical with bushel(s)
76 *higgle* haggle
77 *commodity* could mean 'whore' or 'female pudenda'
80 *chapman* customer   82 *bargain's* Q2 (bargain is Q1)
83 *guinea* then worth 20*s*
85 *chicken* Q2 (you shall bring home the chickens Q1)
88 *ravelin* in fortification, outwork consisting of two faces forming a
salient angle, beyond main ditch and curtain
89 *palisado* one of a row of pointed stakes, an infantry defence
against cavalry

78–9 *I can . . . fourpence.* A groat being worth fourpence; 'probably a
rustic proverb' (Strauss). Cf. 'As like as four pence to a groat': Tilley
F623.

KITE

Why 'tis like a modern minced pie, but the crust is confounded hard, and the plums are somewhat hard of
digestion!

BULLOCK

Then your palisado, pray what may he be? – Come, Ruose,   95
pray ha' done.

KITE

Your palisado is a pretty sort of bodkin about the thickness
of my leg.

BULLOCK

(*Aside*) – That's a fib, I believe. – Eh, where's Ruose?
Ruose! Ruose! 'sflesh, where's Ruose gone?   100

KITE

She's gone with the captain.

BULLOCK

The captain! Wauns, there's no pressing of women, sure?

KITE

But there is, sir.

BULLOCK

If the captain should press Ruose, I should be ruined;
which way went she? – Oh, the devil take your rablins and   105
palisaders.   *Exit*

KITE

You shall be better acquainted with them, honest Bullock, or
I shall miss of my aim.

Enter WORTHY

WORTHY

Why, thou'rt the most useful fellow in nature to your
captain, admirable in your way, I find.   110

KITE

Yes, sir, I understand my business, I will say it; you must
know, sir, I was born a gypsy, and bred among that crew till
I was ten year old, there I learned canting and lying; I was
bought from my mother Cleopatra by a certain nobleman
for three pistoles, who liking my beauty made me his page,   115
there I learned impudence and pimping; I was turned off for
wearing my lord's linen, and drinking my lady's ratafia; and
then turned bailiff's follower, there I learned bullying and

115 *pistoles* Q2 (pistols Q1) Spanish gold coins worth about 18*s.*, or
    Scottish £12 pieces, in England worth about £1
117 *ratafia* Q2 (brandy Q1)

swearing. I at last got into the army, and there I learned
whoring and drinking. – So that if your worship pleases to   120
cast up the whole sum, viz., canting, lying, impudence,
pimping, bullying, swearing, whoring, drinking, and a
halberd, you will find the sum total will amount to a
recruiting sergeant.

WORTHY

And pray, what induced you to turn soldier?   125

KITE

Hunger and ambition – the fears of starving and hopes of a
truncheon led me along to a gentleman with a fair tongue
and fair periwig, who loaded me with promises; but I gad
'twas the lightest load that I ever felt in my life – he
promised to advance me, and indeed he did so – to a garret   130
in the Savoy. I asked him why he put me in prison; he called
me lying dog, and said I was in garrison; and indeed 'tis a
garrison that may hold out till doomsday before I should
desire to take it again. But here comes Justice Balance.

Enter BALANCE *and* BULLOCK

BALANCE

Here, you Sergeant, where's your captain? Here's a poor,   135
foolish fellow comes clamouring to me with a complaint, that
your captain has pressed his sister; do you know anything of
this matter, Worthy?

WORTHY

Ha, ha, ha, I know his sister is gone with Plume to his
lodgings to sell him some chickens.   140

BALANCE

Is that all? The fellow's a fool.

BULLOCK

I know that, an't please you; but if your worship pleases to
grant me a warrant to bring her before you for fear o' th'
worst –

BALANCE

Thou'rt mad, fellow, thy sister's safe enough.   145

KITE (*Aside*)

I hope so too.

---

123 *halberd* combination spear and battle-axe, sergeant's symbol of
    authority
127 *truncheon* baton, symbol of authority
131 *the Savoy* in the Strand, London; then a military barracks and prison
145 *Thou'rt mad* Q2 (Thou art a mad Q1)

WORTHY

Hast thou no more sense, fellow, than to believe that the captain can list women?

BULLOCK

I know not whether they list them, or what they do with them, but I'm sure they carry as many women as men with   150
them out of the country.

BALANCE

But how came you not to go along with your sister?

BULLOCK

Luord, sir, I thought no more of her going than I do of the day I shall die; but this gentleman here, not suspecting any hurt neither, I believe – you thought no harm, friend, did ye?   155

KITE

Lack-a-day, sir, not I. – (*Aside*) Only that I believe I shall marry her tomorrow.

BALANCE

I begin to smell powder. Well, friend, but what did that gentleman with you?

BULLOCK

Why, sir, he entertained me with a fine story of a great fight   160
between the Hungarians, I think it was, and the Irish.

KITE

And so, sir, while we were in the heat of the battle, the captain carried off the baggage.

BALANCE

Sergeant, go along with this fellow to your captain, give him my humble service, and desire him to discharge the wench,   165
though he has listed her.

BULLOCK

Aye – and if he ben't free for that, he shall have another man in her place.

162–3 assigned to KITE Ed. (part of BULLOCK's speech Q)
165 *and desire* Q2 (and I desire Q1)

160–1 *a great . . . Irish.* Not impossible, between Hungarians in Eugene's army and Irish regiments in the French service, that fought at Blenheim; but 'Hungarians' may be Bullock's mistake for 'hussars' (see l. 87). Later C18 editions 'improve' to 'a great sea-fight between the Hungarians and the wild Irish'.

162–3 *And . . . baggage.* The assigning of this speech to Kite in later C18 editions is clearly right: it exhibits both his command of military idiom and his brand of humour.

KITE

Come, honest friend. – (*Aside*) You shall go to my quarters
instead of the captain's. *Exeunt* KITE *and* BULLOCK 170

BALANCE

We must get this mad captain his complement of men, and
send him a-packing, else he'll overrun the country.

WORTHY

You see, sir, how little he values your daughter's disdain.

BALANCE

I like him the better; I was much such another fellow at his
age; I never set my heart upon any woman so much as to 175
make me uneasy at the disappointment; but what was very
surprising both to myself and friends, I changed o' th' sudden
from the most fickle lover to the most constant husband in the
world. But how goes your affair with Melinda?

WORTHY

Very slowly. Cupid had formerly wings, but I think in this 180
age he goes upon crutches, or I fancy Venus had been
dallying with her cripple Vulcan when my amour com-
menced, which has made it go on so lamely. My mistress has
got a captain too, but such a captain! As I live, yonder he
comes. 185

BALANCE

Who? That bluff fellow in the sash? I don't know him.

WORTHY

But I engage he knows you, and everybody at first sight; his
impudence were a prodigy, were not his ignorance pro-
portionable; he has the most universal acquaintance of any
man living, for he won't be alone, and nobody will keep him 190
company twice; then he's a Caesar among the women, *veni,
vidi, vici*, that's all. If he has but talked with the maid, he
swears he has lain with the mistress; but the most surprising

178 *to the* Q2 (to be the Q1)
181 *had* Q2 (has Q1)
186 *sash* worn around the waist by some officers
191–2 *veni, vidi, vici* 'I came, I saw, I conquered'; Julius Caesar,
after defeating Pharnaces at Zela

184–5 *yonder he comes.* Q1 provides no stage-direction. N.T.: 'Brazen is
glimpsed crossing the stage, at rear. He disappears [right], only to make
another "subliminal" entrance and exit, crossing [left] to [right], before
re-entering [left] and spotting Worthy. This triple entrance helps to
establish the man's total vagueness and inability to concentrate on
anything for more than a few moments' (Tynan).

part of his character is his memory, which is the most
prodigious, and the most trifling in the world.   195

BALANCE

I have met with such men, and I take this good-for-nothing
memory to proceed from a certain contexture of the brain,
which is purely adapted to impertinencies, and there they
lodge secure, the owner having no thoughts of his own to
disturb them. I have known a man as perfect as a chronologer   200
as to the day and year of most important transactions, but be
altogether ignorant of the causes, springs, or consequences
of any one thing of moment; I have known another acquire
so much by travel, as to tell you the names of most places in
Europe, with their distances of miles, leagues, or hours, as   205
punctually as a post-boy; but for anything else, as ignorant
as the horse that carries the mail.

WORTHY

This is your man, sir, add but the traveller's privilege of
lying, and even that he abuses; this is the picture, behold the
life!   210

Enter BRAZEN

BRAZEN

Mr Worthy, I'm your servant, and so forth – hark'ee, my
dear –

WORTHY

Whispering, sir, before company is not manners, and when
nobody's by, 'tis foolish.

BRAZEN

Company! *Mort de ma vie*, I beg the gentleman's pardon,   215
who is he?

WORTHY

Ask him.

BRAZEN

So I will. – My dear, I'm your servant, and so forth, – your
name, my dear?

BALANCE

Very laconic, sir.   220

BRAZEN

Laconic, a very good name truly; I have known several of
the Laconics abroad. Poor Jack Laconic! He was killed at

206 *punctually* accurately
215 *Mort de ma vie* 'death of my life', softened oath, from 'Mort de
   Dieu'

the battle of Landen. I remember that he had a blue ribband in his hat that very day, and after he fell, we found a piece of neat's tongue in his pocket.   225

BALANCE

Pray, sir, did the French attack us or we them at Landen?

BRAZEN

The French attack us! Oons, sir, are you a Jacobite?

BALANCE

Why that question?

BRAZEN

Because none but a Jacobite could think that the French durst attack us – no, sir, we attacked them on the – I have   230
reason to remember the time, for I had two-and-twenty horses killed under me that day.

WORTHY

Then, sir, you must have rid mighty hard.

BALANCE

Or perhaps, sir, like my countryman, you rid upon half a dozen horses at once.   235

BRAZEN

What d'e mean, gentlemen? I tell you they were killed, all torn to pieces by cannon-shot, except six that I staked to death upon the enemy's *chevaux de frise*.

BALANCE

Noble Captain, may I crave your name?

BRAZEN

Brazen, at your service.   240

BALANCE

Oh, Brazen, a very good name, I have known several of the Brazens abroad.

WORTHY

Do you know Captain Plume, sir?

BRAZEN

Is he anything related to Frank Plume in Northamptonshire?

225 *neat's tongue* ox tongue, a favourite snack
227 *Jacobite* supporter of the dynastic claims of 'James III', the Old Pretender
233 *must have rid* Q2 (rid Q1)
234–51 Perhaps the equestrian Evans; see my 'Some Notes'.
238 *chevaux de frise* instruments for repelling cavalry charges, composed of a joist bristling with iron-pointed spears

223 *Landen.* The French attacked William III's army at Landen, about 30 miles south-east of Brussels, on 29 July 1693, and drove it back after a long, bitter fight.

– Honest Frank! Many, many a dry bottle have we cracked   245
hand to fist; you must have known his brother Charles that
was concerned in the India Company, he married the
daughter of old Tongue-Pad, the Master in Chancery, a very
pretty woman, only squinted a little; she died in childbed of
her first child, but the child survived, 'twas a daughter, but   250
whether 'twas called Margaret or Marjory, upon my soul I
can't remember – but, gentlemen (*looking on his watch*), I
must meet a lady, a twenty-thousand-pounder, presently,
upon the walk by the water – Worthy, your servant; Laconic,
yours.   *Exit*   255

BALANCE

If you can have so mean an opinion of Melinda, as to be
jealous of this fellow, I think she ought to give you cause to
be so.

WORTHY

I don't think she encourages him so much for gaining herself
a lover, as to set me up a rival; were there any credit to be   260
given to his words, I should believe Melinda had made him
this assignation; I must go see – sir, you'll pardon me.

BALANCE

Aye, aye, sir, you're a man of business.   [*Exit* WORTHY]
But what have we got here?

Enter ROSE *singing*

ROSE

And I shall be a lady, a captain's lady, and ride single upon   265
a white horse with a star, upon a velvet sidesaddle; and I
shall go to London and see the tombs and the lions, and the
Queen. Sir, an't please your worship, I have often seen your
worship ride through our grounds a-hunting, begging your
worship's pardon – pray, what may this lace be worth a yard?   270
                                        Showing some lace

---

248 *Tongue-Pad* talkative person, esp. if smooth and insinuating
248 *Master in Chancery* one of the twelve assistants to the Lord
      Chancellor
264 s.d. *singing* Q2 (*singing what she pleases* Q1)

---

267 *the tombs and the lions.* 'The three great sights of London [were] the lions
      at the Tower, the tombs in Westminster Abbey, and the poor mad folk
      in Bedlam. "To see the lions" is proverbial, and these had to be visited
      by every one new to the City' (Ashton, p. 186; see *Tatler*, No. 30,
      Spectator, No. 26).

BALANCE

Right Mechlin, by this light! Where did you get this lace, child?

ROSE

No matter for that, sir, I come honestly by't.

BALANCE

I question it much.

ROSE

And see here, sir, a fine turkey-shell snuff-box, and fine   275
mangeree, see here: (*takes snuff affectedly*) the captain learnt
me how to take it with an air.

BALANCE

Oho, the captain! Now the murder's out – and so the
captain taught you to take it with an air?

ROSE

Yes, and give it with an air too – will your worship please to   280
taste my snuff?   *Offers the box affectedly*

BALANCE

You're a very apt scholar, pretty maid. And pray what did
you give the captain for these fine things?

ROSE

He's to have my brother for a soldier, and two or three sweethearts that I have in the country, they shall all go with the   285
captain. Oh, he's the finest man, and the humblest withal;
would you believe it, sir? he carried me up with him to his
own chamber with as much familiarity as if I had been the
best lady in the land.

271 *Mechlin* type of lace made in Mechlin in Belgium
275 *turkey-shell* presumably 'tortoise shell', or 'turtle shell', mis-
    remembered
276 *mangeree* presumably 'orangery' misremembered: a snuff scented
    with an extract from orange flowers
    s.d. *takes* Q2 (*She takes* Q1)

276 *takes snuff affectedly*. 'The Exercise of the Snuff Box, according to the
    most fashionable Airs and Motions', by both sexes, is satirized in
    Spectators 138 and 344. The fad arose in England following the capture
    of a huge amount of Spanish snuff in 1702.

BALANCE
    Oh, he's a mighty familiar gentleman as can be.   290

               Enter PLUME *singing*

PLUME
               But it is not so
               With those that go
               Through frost and snow
               Most apropos,
               My maid with the milking-pail.   295

                        Takes hold on ROSE

How, the justice! Then I'm arraigned, condemned, and executed.

BALANCE
    Oh, my noble Captain.

ROSE
    And my noble captain too, sir.

PLUME
    'Sdeath, child, are you mad? – Mr Balance, I am so full of   300
business about my recruits, that I han't a moment's time to –
I have just now three or four people to –

BALANCE
    Nay, Captain, I must speak to you.

ROSE
    And so must I too, Captain.

PLUME
    Any other time, sir – I cannot for my life, sir –   305

BALANCE
    Pray, sir.

PLUME
    Twenty thousand things – I would but – now, sir, pray –
devil take me – I cannot – I must –   *Breaks away*

BALANCE
    Nay, I'll follow you.   *Exit*

ROSE
    And I too.   *Exit*   310

290 f. be/*Enter* Q2 (Q1 reads:
    ROSE
        But I must beg your worship's pardon, I must go seek out my
        brother Bullock.   *Runs off singing*
    BALANCE
        If all officers took the same method of recruiting with this
        gentleman, they might come in time to be fathers as well as cap-
        tains of their companies.)

291–5 Lines from a well-known song, 'The Milkmaid's Life', see Appendix 2.

[Act III], Scene ii

The Walk by the Severn side
Enter MELINDA *and her maid* LUCY

MELINDA

And pray, was it a ring, or buckle, or pendants, or knots; or
in what shape was the almighty gold transformed that has
bribed you so much in his favour?

LUCY

Indeed, madam, the last bribe I had was from the captain,
and that was only a small piece of Flanders edging for   5
pinners.

MELINDA

Aye, Flanders lace is as constant a present from officers to
their women as something else is from their women to them.
They every year bring over a cargo of lace to cheat the
Queen of her duty, and her subjects of their honesty.   10

LUCY

They only barter one sort of prohibited goods for another,
madam.

MELINDA

Has any of them been bartering with you, Mrs Pert, that you
talk so like a trader?

LUCY

Madam, you talk as peevishly to me as if it were my fault,   15
the crime is none of mine though I pretend to excuse it;
though he should not see you this week, can I help it? But as
I was saying, madam, his friend Captain Plume has so taken
him up these two days –

MELINDA

Psha! Would his friend, the captain, were tied upon his back; 20
I warrant he has never been sober since that confounded
captain came to town; the devil take all officers, I say – they
do the nation more harm by debauching us at home, than
they do good by defending us abroad: no sooner a captain
comes to town, but all the young fellows flock about him,   25
and we can't keep a man to ourselves.

1 *knots* bows of ribbon (of gold thread?)
6 *pinners* cap-like headdress with two long flaps
14 *trader* whore
20 *tied . . . back* as a monkey would be tied on a donkey's back, to be
   attacked by dogs, as a comic interlude at the Bear Gardens

LUCY

One would imagine, madam, by your concern for Worthy's absence, that you should use him better when he's with you.

MELINDA

Who told you, pray, that I was concerned for his absence? I'm only vexed that I've had nothing said to me these two   30
days: one may like the love and despise the lover, I hope; as one may love the treason and hate the traitor. Oh! Here comes another captain, and a rogue that has the confidence to make love to me; but indeed I don't wonder at that, when he has the assurance to fancy himself a fine gentleman.   35

LUCY (*Aside*)

If he should speak o' th' assignation, I should be ruined.

Enter BRAZEN

BRAZEN

True to the touch, faith. (*Aside*) I'll draw up all my compliments into one grand platoon, and fire upon her at once.
Thou peerless princess of Salopian plains,
Envied by nymphs and worshipped by the swains,   40
Behold how humbly does the Severn glide,
To greet thee, princess of the Severn side.
Madam, I'm your humble servant and all that, madam – a fine river this same Severn – do you love fishing, madam?

MELINDA

'Tis a pretty melancholy amusement for lovers.   45

BRAZEN

I'll go buy hooks and lines presently; for you must know, madam, that I have served in Flanders against the French, in Hungary against the Turks, and in Tangier against the Moors, and I was never so much in love before; and split me, madam, in all the campaigns I ever made I have not seen so   50
fine a woman as your ladyship.

32 *treason . . . traitor* proverbial. Tilley, K64
33 *confidence* impudence
37 *touch* test
37–42 so, Q1 (all after 'faith' omitted, Q2)
38 *platoon* small group of foot-soldiers, drilled as a unit

39–42 Brazen's use of the quatrain, with Plume's later, serves to emphasize its triteness.
48 *in Hungary*. The Imperialist armies drove the Turks out of Hungary finally in 1697.
Tangier. The English garrisoned Tangier between 1661 and 1683.

MELINDA

And from all the men I ever saw I never had so fine a
compliment; but you soldiers are the best-bred men, that
we must allow.

BRAZEN

Some of us, madam, but there are brutes among us too, very   55
sad brutes; for my own part, I have always had the good luck
to prove agreeable – I have had very considerable offers,
madam, I might have married a German princess worth fifty
thousand crowns a year, but her stove disgusted me. – The
daughter of a Turkish bashaw fell in love with me too when   60
I was prisoner among the infidels; she offered to rob her
father of his treasure, and make her escape with me, but I
don't know how, my time was not come; hanging and
marriage, you know, go by destiny; Fate has reserved me
for a Shropshire lady with twenty thousand pound – do   65
you know any such person, madam?

MELINDA

Extravagant coxcomb! – To be sure, a great many ladies of
that fortune would be proud of the name of Mrs Brazen.

BRAZEN

Nay, for that matter, madam, there are women of very good
quality of the name of Brazen.   70

Enter WORTHY

MELINDA

Oh, are you there, gentleman? – Come, Captain, we'll walk
this way, give me your hand.

---

56 *sad* deplorably bad
60 *bashaw* pasha
63–4 *hanging . . . destiny* proverbial. Tilley, W232

---

59 *her stove* (a) Sitting-room or bedroom heated with a furnace; or (b)
foot-warmer containing burning charcoal, which Dutch women tucked
under their skirts; or possibly (c) sweating-room. In William Cavendish's *The Humorous Lovers* (1677), p. 10, it is said of the character
Furrs, obsessive about keeping warm, that 'A *Dutch* Stove would make
him a most passionate Lover'. The sense here is probably the first.
Jeffares notes that 'English travellers often objected to the overheating
of rooms on the continent'. In Augustin Daly's stage-version of the
play, 'but her stove disgusted me' is replaced by: ' "but the garlic and
onions! Whew!" perhaps from some old prompt-book' (Strauss).

BRAZEN

My hand, heart's blood, and guts are at your service. –
Mr Worthy – your servant, my dear. *Exit leading* MELINDA

WORTHY

Death and fire! This is not to be borne.   75

Enter PLUME

PLUME

No more it is, faith.

WORTHY

What?

PLUME

The March beer at the Raven; I have been doubly serving
the Queen, – raising men and raising the excise – recruiting
and elections are rare friends to the excise.   80

WORTHY

You an't drunk?

PLUME

No, no, whimsical only; I could be mighty foolish, and
fancy myself mighty witty; Reason still keeps its throne,
but it nods a little, that's all.

WORTHY

Then you're just fit for a frolic?   85

PLUME

As fit as close pinners for a punk in the pit.

WORTHY

There's your play then, recover me that vessel from that
Tangerine.

PLUME

She's well rigged, but how is she manned?

WORTHY

By Captain Brazen that I told you of today; she is called   90
the Melinda, a first rate I can assure you; she sheered off
with him just now on purpose to affront me, but according

78 *March beer* strong beer brewed in March
80 *rare* Q2 (good Q1)
83–4 *Reason . . . little* cf. proverb, 'Let reason rule all your actions',
Tilley R43
86 *punk in the pit* whore in the pit of the theatre
88 *Tangerine* Tangiers privateer or pirate ship
89 *rigged* pun on slang sense, 'clothed'
90 *she* Q2 (the frigate Q1)
91 *first rate* warship of the highest rating

to your advice I would take no notice, because I would
seem to be above a concern for her behaviour. But have a
care of a quarrel.   95

PLUME
No, no, I never quarrel with anything in my cups but an
oyster wench or a cook maid, and if they ben't civil, I knock
'em down. But hark'ee my friend, I will make love, and I
must make love. I tell'ee what, I'll make love like a platoon.

WORTHY
Platoon, how's that?   100

PLUME
I'll kneel, stoop, and stand, faith; most ladies are gained by
platooning.

WORTHY
Here they come; I must leave you.   *Exit*

PLUME
So – now must I look as sober and demure as a whore at a
christening.   105

Enter BRAZEN *and* MELINDA

BRAZEN
Who's that, madam?

MELINDA
A brother officer of yours, I suppose, sir.

BRAZEN
Aye! – (*To* PLUME) My dear.

PLUME
My dear!   *They run and embrace*

BRAZEN
My dear boy, how is't? – Your name, my dear? If I be not   110
mistaken, I have seen your face.

PLUME
I never see yours in my life, my dear – but there's a face

 96 *but an* Q2 (but with an Q1)
100 *Platoon* Q2 (A platoon Q1)
104 *must I* Q2 (I must Q1)
107 *sir* Q2 (not in Q1)

101 *kneel, stoop, and stand.* Musketeers were drilled to fire in all three posi-
    tions, so that a platoon drawn up in three or more ranks could fire a
    single massed volley; or else, kneel to reload, while the ranks behind
    fired over their heads, for continuous volley-firing. See A. R., *The
    Accomplished Officer*, trans. from French (2nd edition, 1708), p. 191.

well known as the sun's, that shines on all and is by all
adored.

BRAZEN

Have you any pretensions, sir?   115

PLUME

Pretensions!

BRAZEN

That is, sir, have you ever served abroad?

PLUME

I have served at home, sir, for ages served this cruel fair –
and that will serve the turn, sir.

MELINDA (*Aside*)

So, between the fool and the rake I shall bring a fine spot of   120
work upon my hands – I see Worthy yonder, I could be
content to be friends with him would he come this way.

BRAZEN

Will you fight for the lady, sir?

PLUME

No, sir, but I'll have her notwithstanding.
    Thou peerless princess of Salopian plains,   125
    Envied by nymphs and worshipped by the swains—

BRAZEN

Oons, sir, not fight for her!

PLUME

Prithee be quiet, I shall be out –
        Behold how humbly does the Severn glide
        To greet thee, princess of the Severn side.   130

BRAZEN

Don't mind him, madam. – If he were not so well dressed I
should take him for a poet; but I'll show the difference
presently – come, madam, we'll place you between us, and
now the longest sword carries her.

                              Draws, MELINDA *shrieks*

                    Enter WORTHY

MELINDA

Oh, Mr Worthy, save me from these madmen.   135
                         Runs off with WORTHY

PLUME

Ha, ha, ha, why don't you follow, sir, and fight the bold
ravisher?

113 *sun . . . all* proverbial. Tilley, S985
118 *fair* beauty

BRAZEN
No, sir, you're my man.

PLUME
I don't like the wages, and I won't be your man.

BRAZEN
Then you're not worth my sword.   140

PLUME
No? Pray what did it cost?

BRAZEN
It cost me twenty pistoles in France, and my enemies
thousands of lives in Flanders.

PLUME
Then they had a dear bargain.

Enter SILVIA *dressed in man's apparel*

SILVIA
Save ye, save ye, gentlemen.   145

BRAZEN
My dear, I'm yours.

PLUME
Do you know the gentleman?

BRAZEN
No, but I will presently. – Your name, my dear?

SILVIA
Wilful, Jack Wilful, at your service.

BRAZEN
What! The Kentish Wilfuls or those of Staffordshire?   150

SILVIA
Both, sir, both; I'm related to all the Wilfuls in Europe,
and I'm head of the family at present.

PLUME
Do you live in this country, sir?

SILVIA
Yes, sir, I live where I stand, I have neither home, house,
nor habitation beyond this spot of ground.   155

BRAZEN
What are you, sir?

SILVIA
A rake.

142–3 *It cost . . . Flanders* Q2 (It cost my enemies thousands of lives,
  sir Q1); pun on 'livres'
153 *this* Q2 (the Q1)
154 *stand* Q2 (should Q1)

PLUME

In the army, I presume.

SILVIA

No, but intend to list immediately – look'ee, gentlemen,
he that bids me fairest has me.   160

BRAZEN

Sir, I'll prefer you, I'll make you a corporal this minute.

PLUME

A corporal! I'll make you my companion, you shall eat with
me.

BRAZEN

You shall drink with me.

PLUME

You shall lie with me, you young rogue.   *Kisses her*   165

BRAZEN

You shall receive your pay and do no duty.

SILVIA

Then you must make me a field-officer.

PLUME

Pho, pho, I'll do more than all this, I'll make you a corporal,
and give you a brevet for sergeant.

BRAZEN

Can you read and write, sir?   170

SILVIA

Yes.

BRAZEN

Then your business is done, I'll make you chaplain to the
regiment.

SILVIA

Your promises are so equal that I'm at a loss to choose;
there is one Plume that I hear much commended in town,   175
pray which of you is Captain Plume?

PLUME

I am Captain Plume.

159 *but intend* Q2 (but I intend Q1)
160 *has* Q2 (shall have Q1)
167 *field-officer* officer above the rank of captain and below that of
    general
169 *brevet* document conferring nominal rank
177 *I am* Q2 (I'm Q1)

165 *lie with me.* Sharing beds was the rule rather than the exception; a
century later Wellington's junior officers were sometimes four to a bed.

BRAZEN
No, no, I'm Captain Plume.

SILVIA
Hey day!

PLUME
Captain Plume, I'm your servant, my dear.	180

BRAZEN
Captain Brazen, I'm yours. – The fellow dare not fight.

Enter KITE

KITE
Sir, if you please –	*Goes to whisper* PLUME

PLUME
No, no, there's your captain. – Captain Plume, your sergeant here has got so drunk he mistakes me for you.

BRAZEN
He's an incorrigible sot. – Here, my Hector of Holborn,	185
forty shillings for you.

PLUME
I forbid the banns – look'ee, friend, you shall list with
Captain Brazen.

SILVIA
I will see Captain Brazen hanged first, I will list with
Captain Plume; I'm a freeborn Englishman and will be a	190
slave my own way. – (*To* BRAZEN) Look'ee, sir, will you stand
by me?

BRAZEN
I warrant you, my lad.

SILVIA
Then I will tell you, Captain Brazen (*to* PLUME), that you
are an ignorant, pretending, impudent coxcomb.	195

BRAZEN
Aye, aye, a sad dog.

SILVIA
A very sad dog; give me the money, noble Captain Plume.

178 *I'm* Q2 (I am Q1)

---

185 *Hector of Holborn*. Holborn was the route along which criminals were
taken from Newgate to Tyburn to be hanged; the title probably means
'gallows-bird swashbuckler', formed as an analogue of 'Guy of Hamp-
ton' and other names of heroes of chivalric romance. 'Hectors' were
swaggering ruffians, who infested the London streets and taverns in the
late C17; Holborn was one of their known haunts.
186 *forty shillings*. The bounty for volunteering.

PLUME

Then you won't list with Captain Brazen?

SILVIA

I won't.

BRAZEN

Never mind him, child, I'll end the dispute presently; 200
hark'ee, my dear –

Takes PLUME *to one side of the stage and entertains him in
dumb show*

KITE

Sir, he in the plain coat is Captain Plume; I'm his sergeant
and will take my oath on't.

SILVIA

What! You are Sergeant Kite?

KITE

At your service.   205

SILVIA

Then I would not take your oath for a farthing.

KITE

A very understanding youth of his age! Pray, sir, let me
look you full in the face.

SILVIA

Well, sir, what have you to say to my face?

KITE

The very image and superscription of my brother, two   210
bullets of the same calibre were never so like; sure it must
be Charles, Charles –

SILVIA

What d'ye mean by Charles?

KITE

The voice too, only a little variation in effa ut flat; my dear
brother, for I must call you so, if you should have the   215
fortune to enter into the most noble society of the sword, I
bespeak you for a comrade.

SILVIA

No, sir, I'll be your captain's comrade if anybody's.

198 *Then* Q2 (Hold, hold, then Q1)
204 *You are* Q2 (Are you Q1)
214 *effa ut flat* Q2 (C fa ut flat Q1)

---

214 *effa ut flat.* F fa ut, the fuller name of the note F which was sung to the
    syllable *fa* or *ut* according as it occurred in one or other of the hexa-
    chords to which it could belong (a hexachord being a diatonic series or
    scale of six notes); i.e., the musical key of F minor.

KITE

Ambition! There again, 'tis a noble passion for a soldier; by
that I gained this glorious halberd. Ambition! I see a com-   220
mission in his face already; pray, noble Captain, give me
leave to salute you.   *Offers to kiss her*

SILVIA

What, men kiss one another!

KITE

We officers do, 'tis our way; we live together like man and
wife, always either kissing or fighting. – But I see a storm   225
a-coming.

SILVIA

Now, Sergeant, I shall see who is your captain by your
knocking down the t'other.

KITE

My captain scorns assistance, sir.

BRAZEN

How dare you contend for anything and not dare to draw   230
your sword? But you're a young fellow, and have not been
much abroad, I excuse that; but prithee resign the man,
prithee do; you're a very honest fellow.

PLUME

You lie, and you're a son of a whore.
                    Draws, and makes up to BRAZEN

BRAZEN (*Retiring*)

Hold, hold, did not you refuse to fight for the lady?   235

PLUME

I always do – but for a man I'll fight knee deep, so you lie
again.

   PLUME *and* BRAZEN *fight a traverse or two about the stage;*
   SILVIA *draws, and is held by* KITE, *who sounds to arms with his*
   mouth, takes SILVIA *in his arms, and carries her off the stage*

BRAZEN

Hold – where's the man?

PLUME

Gone.

BRAZEN

Then what do we fight for? (*Puts up*) Now let's embrace,   240
my dear.

---

223 *men kiss.* The practice was generally thought foppish and Frenchified or
   intolerably boorish, but was evidently customary among sergeants (see
   Congreve, *The Way of the World*, III.xv, 72–3).

PLUME

With all my heart, my dear. (*Putting up*) I suppose Kite
has listed him by this time.   *They embrace*

BRAZEN

You're a brave fellow. I always fight with a man before I
make him my friend; and if once I find he will fight, I never   245
quarrel with him afterwards. – And now I'll tell you a
secret, my dear friend, that lady we frighted out o'the walk
just now I found in bed this morning, so beautiful, so
inviting – I presently locked the door – but I'm a man of
honour – but I believe I shall marry her nevertheless; her   250
twenty thousand pound, you know, will be a pretty conveniency – I had an assignation with her here, but your
coming spoiled my sport, curse ye, my dear, – but don't do
so again.

PLUME

No, no, my dear, men are my business at present.   255

                                                      Exeunt

Act IV, Scene i

The Walk by the Severn side
[Enter] ROSE *and* BULLOCK *meeting*

ROSE

Where have you been, you great booby? You're always out
o' th'way in the time of preferment.

BULLOCK

Preferment! Who should prefer me?

ROSE

I would prefer you; who should prefer a man but a woman?
Come throw away that great club, hold up your head,   5
cock your hat, and look big.

BULLOCK

Ah! Ruose, Ruose, I fear somebody will look big sooner
than folk think of; this genteel breeding never comes into
the country without a train of followers. – Here has been
Cartwheel your sweetheart, what will become o' him?   10

ROSE

Look'ee, I'm a great woman and will provide for my rela-

242 s.d. *Putting* Q2 (*Puts* Q1)   247 *lady we* Q2 (lady that we Q1)
251–2 *conveniency* Q2 (convenience Q1)
  0.2 *The Walk . . . side* Ed. (SCENE *of the Walk continues* Q)
  6 *look big* attempt an impressive manner

tions; I told the captain how finely he played upon the
tabor and pipe, so he has set him down for drum-major.

BULLOCK

Nay, sister, why did not you keep that place for me? You
know I always loved to be a-drumming, if it were but on a 15
table, or on a quart pot.

Enter SILVIA

SILVIA

Had I but a commission in my pocket I fancy my breeches
would become me as well as any ranting fellow of 'em all;
for I take a bold step, a rakish toss, a smart cock, and an
impudent air to be the principal ingredients in the com- 20
position of a captain. – What's here? Rose, my nurse's
daughter. I'll go and practise. – Come, child, kiss me at
once. (*Kisses* ROSE) And her brother too. – Well, honest
Dungfork, do you know the difference between a horse cart
and a cart horse, eh? 25

BULLOCK

I presume that your worship is a captain by your clothes
and your courage.

SILVIA

Suppose I were, would you be contented to list, friend?

ROSE

No, no, though your worship be a handsome man, there be
others as fine as you; my brother is engaged to Captain 30
Plume.

SILVIA

Plume! Do you know Captain Plume?

ROSE

Yes, I do, and he knows me. – He took the very ribbands
out of his shirtsleeves and put 'em into my shoes – see
there. – I can assure you that I can do ánything with the 35
captain.

12 *played* Q2 (could play Q1)
13 *tabor* small drum on which the piper accompanied himself
  for drum-major Q2 (for a drum-major Q1)
19 *toss* quick upward or backward movement of the head
19 *cock* upward or significant turn
34 *'em* Q2 (them Q1)   35 *you* Q2 (not in Q1)

---

13 *drum major* NCO in command of the regimental drummers (Scouller,
  pp. 99–100, 377)
24 *horse cart.* 'To set the cart before the horse' (proverb; Tilley C103)
  itself means to reverse the right order.

BULLOCK

That is, in a modest way, sir. – Have a care what you say,
Ruose, don't shame your parentage.

ROSE

Nay, for that matter I am not so simple as to say that I can
do anything with the captain, but what I may do with any-   40
body else.

SILVIA

So! And pray what do you expect from this captain, child?

ROSE

I expect, sir! I expect – but he ordered me to tell nobody –
but suppose that he should promise to marry me?

SILVIA

You should have a care, my dear, men will promise any-   45
thing beforehand.

ROSE

I know that, but he promised to marry me afterwards.

BULLOCK

Wauns, Ruose, what have you said?

SILVIA

Afterwards! After what?

ROSE

After I had sold him my chickens. – I hope there's no   50
harm in that.

Enter PLUME

PLUME

What, Mr Wilful, so close with my market-woman!

SILVIA

(*Aside*) I'll try if he loves her. – Close, sir! aye, and closer
yet, sir. – Come, my pretty maid, you and I will withdraw a
little.   55

PLUME

No, no, friend, I han't done with her yet.

SILVIA

Nor have I begun with her, so I have as good a right as you
have.

51 *that* Q2 (that, though there be an ugly song of chickens and
   sparagus Q1)
56–82 so, Q2 (alternative version in Appendix 1, Q1)

---

51 The 'song' (Q1) has been identified by Peter Dixon as *The three jovial
   companions, or the merry travellers, who paid their shot where ever they
   came, without ever a stiver of money* (ca. 1685), reprinted in *Pills to Purge
   Melancholy,* ed. T. Durfey (1714), V, 17–19. It is decidedly bawdy.

PLUME
Thou art a bloody impudent fellow.

SILVIA
Sir, I would qualify myself for the service.   60

PLUME
Hast thou really a mind to the service?

SILVIA
Yes, sir; so let her go.

ROSE
Pray, gentlemen, don't be so violent.

PLUME
Come, leave it to the girl's own choice. – Will you belong to
me or to that gentleman?   65

ROSE
Let me consider, you're both very handsome.

PLUME
Now the natural inconstancy of her sex begins to work.

ROSE
Pray, sir, what will you give me?

BULLOCK
Don't be angry, sir, that my sister should be mercenary,
for she's but young.   70

SILVIA
Give thee, child! – I'll set thee above scandal; you shall have
a coach with six before and six behind, an equipage to make
vice fashionable, and put virtue out of countenance.

PLUME
Pho, that's easily done, – I'll do more for thee, child, I'll
buy you a furbelow scarf, and give you a ticket to see a play. 75

BULLOCK
A play! Wauns, Ruose, take the ticket, and let's see the
show.

SILVIA
Look'ee, Captain, if you won't resign, I'll go list with
Captain Brazen this minute.

PLUME
Will you list with me if I give up my title?   80

---

72 *coach . . . behind* six horses before, six footmen on the rear
platform
75 *furbelow* flounced

---

59 *bloody*. As an intensive, has at this time an undertone of high but rois-
tering blood.

SILVIA

I will.

PLUME

Take her: I'll change a woman for a man at any time.

ROSE

I have heard before, indeed, that you captains used to sell
your men.

BULLOCK

(*Crying*) Pray, Captain, don't send Ruose to the West   85
Indies.

PLUME

Ha, ha, ha, West Indies! No, no, my honest lad, give me
thy hand; nor you nor she shall move a step farther than I
do. – This gentleman is one of us, and will be kind to you,
Mrs Rose.   90

ROSE

But will you be so kind to me, sir, as the captain would?

SILVIA

I can't be altogether so kind to you, my circumstances are
not so good as the captain's; but I'll take care of you, upon
my word.

PLUME

Aye, aye, we'll all take care of her; she shall live like a   95
princess, and her brother here shall be – what would you be?

BULLOCK

Ah! sir, if you had not promised the place of drum-major –

PLUME

Aye, that is promised – but what think ye of barrack-
master? You're a person of understanding, and barrack-
master you shall be. – But what's become of this same   100
Cartwheel you told me of, my dear?

ROSE

We'll go fetch him – come, brother barrack-master. – We
shall find you at home, noble Captain?

Exeunt ROSE *and* BULLOCK

PLUME

Yes, yes – and now, sir, here are your forty shillings.

83 *used* Q2 (use Q1)

85–6 *West Indies.* Service here was rightly dreaded: 'the men died like
flies from tropical diseases and gross neglect, forgotten by the War
Office and often by their own absentee officers', who, like the civil con-
tractors, were usually defrauding them of pay, food and clothing
(G. M. Trevelyan, *England under Queen Anne: Blenheim* [London,
1948], pp. 217, 228).

SILVIA

Captain Plume, I despise your listing-money; if I do serve,   105
'tis purely for love – of that wench I mean. For you must
know, that among my other sallies, I have spent the best
part of my fortune in search of a maid, and could never
find one hitherto; so you may be assured I'd not sell my
freedom under a less purchase than I did my estate. – So   110
before I list I must be certified that this girl is a virgin.

PLUME

Mr Wilful, I can't tell how you can be certified in that point,
till you try, but upon my honour she may be a vestal for
aught that I know to the contrary. – I gained her heart
indeed by some trifling presents and promises, and knowing   115
that the best security for a woman's soul is her body, I
would have made myself master of that too, had not the
jealousy of my impertinent landlady interposed.

SILVIA

So you only want an opportunity for accomplishing your
designs upon her?   120

PLUME

Not at all, I have already gained my ends, which were only
the drawing in one or two of her followers. The women, you
know, are the loadstones everywhere: gain the wives and
you're caressed by the husbands; please the mistresses and
you are valued by their gallants; secure an interest with the   125
finest women at court and you procure the favour of the
greatest men; so, kiss the prettiest country wenches and
you are sure of listing the lustiest fellows. Some people
may call this artifice, but I term it stratagem, since it is so
main a part of the service – besides, the fatigue of recruiting   130
is so intolerable, that unless we could make ourselves some
pleasure amidst the pain, no mortal man would be able to
bear it.

SILVIA

Well, sir, I'm satisfied as to the point in debate; but now let
me beg you to lay aside your recruiting airs, put on the man   135
of honour, and tell me plainly what usage I must expect when
I'm under your command.

---

109 *I'd not* Ed. (I won't Q1; I'd Q2)
130 *main* highly important   *fatigue* Q2 (fatigues Q1)

---

111 N.T.: 'Insisting on a virgin is of course evidence of lubricity, not prim-
ness. Silvia is trying to pass herself off as a thoroughly jaded rake' (Tynan).

PLUME

You must know in the first place, then, that I hate to have
gentlemen in my company, for they are always troublesome and expensive, sometimes dangerous; and 'tis a con-   140
stant maxim amongst us, that those who know the least
obey the best. Notwithstanding all this, I find something
so agreeable about you, that engages me to court your company; and I can't tell how it is, but I should be uneasy to
see you under the command of anybody else. – Your usage   145
will chiefly depend upon your behaviour; only this you
must expect, that if you commit a small fault I will excuse it,
if a great one, I'll discharge you; for something tells me I
shall not be able to punish you.

SILVIA

And something tells me, that if you do discharge me 'twill be   150
the greatest punishment you can inflict; for were we this
moment to go upon the greatest dangers in your profession,
they would be less terrible to me than to stay behind you. –
And now your hand, – this lists me – and now you are my
captain.   155

PLUME

Your friend. (*Kisses her*) 'Sdeath! There's something in this
fellow that charms me.

SILVIA

One favour I must beg – this affair will make some noise, and
I have some friends that would censure my conduct if I
threw myself into the circumstance of a private sentinel of   160
my own head; I must therefore take care to be impressed by
the Act of Parliament; you shall leave that to me.

PLUME

What you please as to that. – Will you lodge at my quarters
in the meantime? You shall have part of my bed.

SILVIA

Oh, fie, lie with a common soldier! – Would not you rather   165
lie with a common woman?

PLUME

No, faith, I'm not that rake that the world imagines; I have

141 *amongst* Q2 (among Q1)   151 *can* Q2 (will Q1)
160 *circumstance* Q2 (circumstances Q1)
    private sentinel private soldier
167 *I'm* Q2 (I am Q1)

167–73 N.T.: 'This is an honest confession on Plume's part—and he makes
    it to Wilful, the professed rake, with some embarrassment' (Tynan).

got an air of freedom which people mistake for lewdness in
me, as they mistake formality in others for religion; the
world is all a cheat, only I take mine which is undesigned to   170
be more excusable than theirs, which is hypocritical; I hurt
nobody but myself, and they abuse all mankind. – Will you
lie with me?

SILVIA

No, no, Captain, you forget Rose, she's to be my bedfellow
you know.   175

PLUME

I had forgot, pray be kind to her.   *Exeunt severally*

Enter MELINDA *and* LUCY

MELINDA

'Tis the greatest misfortune in nature for a woman to want a
confidante: we are so weak that we can do nothing without
assistance, and then a secret racks us worse than the colic;
I'm at this minute so sick of a secret that I'm ready to faint   180
away – help me, Lucy.

LUCY

Bless me, madam, what's the matter?

MELINDA

Vapours only – I begin to recover – if Silvia were in town, I
could heartily forgive her faults for the ease of discovering
my own.   185

LUCY

You're thoughtful, madam; am not I worthy to know the
cause?

MELINDA

You're a servant, and a secret would make you saucy.

LUCY

Not unless you should find fault without a cause, madam.

MELINDA

Cause or not cause, I must not lose the pleasure of chiding
when I please; women must discharge their vapours some-
where, and before we get husbands, our servants must
expect to bear with 'em.

LUCY

Then, madam, you had better raise me to a degree above a
servant: you know my family, and that five hundred pound   195
would set me upon the foot of a gentlewoman, and make me
worthy the confidence of any lady in the land. Besides,

169 *formality* mere compliance with forms   172 *and* Q2 (but Q1)
176 *Hunt and Archer start a new scene here*

madam, 'twill extremely encourage me in the great design I
now have in hand.

MELINDA

I don't find that your design can be of any great advantage   200
to you; 'twill please me indeed in the humour I have of being
revenged on the fool for his vanity of making love to me, so
I don't much care if I do promise you five hundred pound
upon my day of marriage.

LUCY

That is the way, madam, to make me diligent in the vocation   205
of a confidante, which I think is generally to bring people
together.

MELINDA

Oh, Lucy, I can hold my secret no longer – you must know
that hearing of the famous fortune-teller in town, I went
disguised to satisfy a curiosity which has cost me dear; that   210
fellow is certainly the devil, or one of his bosom favourites,
he has told me the most surprising things of my past life –

LUCY

Things past, madam, can hardly be reckoned surprising,
because we know them already; did he tell you anything
surprising that was to come?   215

MELINDA

One thing very surprising, he said I should die a maid.

LUCY

Die a maid! Come into the world for nothing! – Dear
madam, if you should believe him, it might come to pass;
for the bare thought on't might kill one in four and twenty
hours. – And did you ask him any questions about me?   220

MELINDA

You! Why, I passed for you.

LUCY

So 'tis I that am to die a maid – but the devil was a liar from
the beginning, he can't make me die a maid – I have put it
out of his power already.

MELINDA

I do but jest, I would have passed for you, and called myself   225
Lucy, but he presently told me my name, my quality, my
fortune, and gave me the whole history of my life; he told me
of a lover I had in this country, and described Worthy
exactly, but in nothing so well as in his present indifference
– I fled to him for refuge here today – he never so much as   230

198 *design I* Q2 (design that I Q1)
204 *upon my day of* Q2 (the day of my Q1)

encouraged me in my fright, but coldly told me that he was
sorry for the accident, because it might give the town cause
to censure my conduct; excused his not waiting on me home,
made me a careless bow, and walked off. 'Sdeath, I could have
stabbed him, or myself, 'twas the same thing. – Yonder he   235
comes – I will so slave him.

LUCY

Don't exasperate him, consider what the fortune-teller told
you; men are scarce, and as times go, it is not impossible for
a woman to die a maid.

Enter WORTHY

MELINDA

No matter.   240

WORTHY

I find she's warmed, I must strike while the iron is hot. –
You have a great deal of courage, madam, to venture into the
walks where you were so late frighted.

MELINDA

And you have a quantity of impudence to appear before me,
that you have so lately affronted.   245

WORTHY

I had no design to affront you, nor appear before you either,
madam; I left you here because I had business in another
place, and came hither thinking to meet another person.

MELINDA

Since you find yourself disappointed, I hope you'll withdraw
to another part of the walk.   250

WORTHY

The walk is broad enough for us both. (*They walk by one
another, he with his hat cocked, she fretting and tearing her fan*)
Will you please to take snuff, madam?
*He offers her his box, she strikes it out of his hand; while he is
gathering it up,*

Enter BRAZEN

BRAZEN

What, here before me, my dear!
Takes MELINDA *round the waist*

241 *strike . . . hot* proverbial. Tilley, I 94
251 *The walk . . . both* Q2 (The walk is as free for me as you, madam,
     and broad enough for us both Q1)
251–2 s.d. so, Hunt (*continuous, following* snuff, madam Q1)
252–3 s.d. *Enter* BRAZEN/*Takes . . . waist* Ed. (*Enter* BRAZEN *who takes*
     MELINDA *about the middle* Q1 ; BRAZEN *takes her round the waist* Q2)

MELINDA

What means this insolence? *She cuffs him*

LUCY

(*To* BRAZEN) Are you mad? Don't you see Mr Worthy? 255

BRAZEN

No, no, I'm struck blind – Worthy! – Adso, well turned, my mistress has wit at her fingers' ends – madam, I ask your pardon, 'tis our way abroad – Mr Worthy, you're the happy man.

WORTHY

I don't envy your happiness very much, if the lady can afford 260 no other sort of favours but what she has bestowed upon you.

MELINDA

I'm sorry the favour miscarried, for it was designed for you, Mr Worthy; and be assured, 'tis the last and only favour you must expect at my hands. – Captain, I ask your pardon. 265

Exit with LUCY

BRAZEN

I grant it. – You see, Mr Worthy, 'twas only a random shot, it might ha' taken off your head as well as mine; courage, my dear, 'tis the fortune of war; but the enemy has thought fit to withdraw, I think.

WORTHY

Withdraw! Oons, sir, what d'ye mean by withdraw? 270

BRAZEN

I'll show you. *Exit*

WORTHY

She's lost, irrecoverably lost, and Plume's advice has ruined me; 'sdeath, why should I that knew her haughty spirit be ruled by a man that's a stranger to her pride.

Enter PLUME

PLUME

Ha, ha, ha, a battle royal; don't frown so, man, she's your 275 own, I tell'ee; I saw the fury of her love in the extremity of

255 s.d. *To* BRAZEN Q2 (*Runs to* BRAZEN Q1)
256 *Adso* exclamation of asseveration   274 *that's* Q2 (that is Q1)

256–8 Brazen pretends to be the recipient of a blow of wit, 'well fashioned', playing on proverbial phrases 'to have wit at will' and 'to have something at one's fingers' ends'—(Tilley, W552, F245) Shugrue makes 'Mr Worthy, you're the happy man' a question; even then these words, with Worthy's reply, remain obscure.

her passion, the wildness of her anger is a certain sign that
she loves you to madness. That rogue, Kite, began the
battle with abundance of conduct, and will bring you off
victorious, my life on't; he plays his part admirably; she's to   280
be with him again presently.

WORTHY
But what could be the meaning of Brazen's familiarity with
her?

PLUME
You are no logician if you pretend to draw consequences
from the actions of fools; there's no arguing by the rule of   285
reason upon a science without principles, and such is their
conduct; whim, unaccountable whim, hurries 'em on, like a
man drunk with brandy before ten o'clock in the morning –
but we lose our sport; Kite has opened above an hour ago,
let's away.   *Exeunt*   290

[Act IV], Scene ii

A Chamber

KITE, *disguised in a strange habit, sitting at a table,* [*whereon are
books and globes;* SERVANT *in attendance*]

KITE (*Rising*)
By the position of the heavens, gained from my observation
upon these celestial globes, I find that Luna was a tide-waiter,
Sol a surveyor, Mercury a thief, Venus a whore, Saturn an
alderman, Jupiter a rake, and Mars a sergeant of grenadiers;
and this is the system of Kite the conjurer.   5

Enter PLUME *and* WORTHY

PLUME
Well, what success?

KITE
I have sent away a shoemaker and a tailor already, one's to be

279 *conduct* skill in managing affairs
287 *'em* Q2 (them Q1)
    0.3 s.d. *A Chamber* Ed. (*A Chamber with books and globes* Q) pres-
    umably within Kite's quarters; see I.i, 130–3
    0.2 s.d. *a strange habit* the German doctor's habit; see I.i, 127–8
    s.d. *habit . . . table* Q2 (*habit, and sitting at the table* Q1)
    2 *tide-waiter* customs official
    3 *surveyor* supervisor of customs officials
      Saturn associated with law and order   5 *system* body of doctrine
    7 *tailor* proverbially cowardly and insignificant (Tilley, T17–25)

a captain of marines and the other a major of dragoons, I am
to manage them at night. Have you seen the lady, Mr
Worthy? 10

WORTHY

Aye, but it won't do – have you showed her her name that I
tore off from the bottom of the letter?

KITE

No, sir, I reserve that for the last stroke.

PLUME

What letter?

WORTHY

One that I would not let you see, for fear you should break 15
windows in good earnest. *Knocking at the door*

KITE

Officers to your post. *Exeunt* WORTHY *and* PLUME
Tycho, mind the door.

SERVANT *opens the door, enter* [THOMAS,] *a* SMITH

SMITH

Well, master, are you the cunning man?

KITE

I am the learned Copernicus. 20

SMITH

Well, Master Coppernose, I'm but a poor man and I can't
afford above a shilling for my fortune.

KITE

Perhaps that is more than 'tis worth.

15–16 *break* Q2 (break Melinda's Q1); cf. III.i, 41
18 *Tycho* (omitted Q2) ex. Tycho Brahe (1546–1601), Danish
   astronomer
19 *cunning* possessing magical knowledge
20 *Copernicus* (1473–1543), Polish astronomer

---

16 *earnest*. Later C18 editions add: 'Here, captain, put it in your pocket-
   book, and have it ready upon occasion'. As Strauss says, 'the purpose of
   this speech evidently was to prepare for the farcical devil scene of Q1';
   see l.237 n.
17 s.d. Hunt's edition has Worthy and Plume retire behind a screen,
   evidently following stage-tradition. This blocking has obvious merits;
   but in Restoration comedies characters offstage, and overhearing, are
   generally in closets, or, as in Vanbrugh's *Provoked Wife*, cupboards.
21 *Coppernose*. Red nose due to disease or intemperance. Rothstein suggests the smith's blunder may be 'Farquhar's mischievous reminiscence
   of Tycho Brahe's famed golden nose' (p. 129). 'Coppernose' was
   omitted in Q2, perhaps as too farcical.

SMITH

Look'ee, doctor, let me have something that's good for my
shilling, or I'll have my money again.   25

KITE

If there be faith in the stars, you shall have your shilling forty
fold. Your hand, countryman – you are by trade a smith.

SMITH

How the devil should you know that?

KITE

Because the devil and you are brother tradesmen – you were
born under Forceps.   30

SMITH

Forceps, what's that?

KITE

One of the signs; there's Leo, Sagittarius, Forceps, Furnes,
Dixmude, Namur, Brussels, Charleroi, and so forth – twelve
of 'em. Let me see – did you ever make any bombs or
cannon-bullets?   35

SMITH

Not I.

KITE

You either have, or will – the stars have decreed that you
shall be – I must have more money, sir, your fortune's great –

SMITH

Faith, doctor, I have no more.

KITE

Oh, sir, I'll trust you, and take it out of your arrears.   40

SMITH

Arrears! What arrears?

KITE

The five hundred pound that's owing to you from the
government.

SMITH

Owing me!

---

30 *Forceps* obstetrical instrument, smith's tongs
32 *Furnes* of these Flanders towns, this fell to the French, January
    1693
33 *Dixmude* fell to the French, July 1695
33 *Namur* fell to the French, June 1692, recaptured in September
    1695
33 *Brussels* William frustrated a French attack, 1697
    Charleroi fell to the French, 1693
35 *cannon* Q2 (cannons Q1)
40 *arrears* See Appendix 5.

KITE

Owing you, sir – let me see your t'other hand – I beg your   45
pardon, it will be owing to you; and the rogue of an agent
will demand fifty per cent for a fortnight's advance.

SMITH

I'm in the clouds, doctor, all this while.

KITE

Sir, I am above 'em, among the stars – in two years, three
months, and two hours, you will be made Captain of the   50
Forges to the Grand Train of Artillery, and will have ten
shillings a day and two servants; 'tis the decree of the stars,
and of the fixed stars, that are as immovable as your anvil.
Strike, sir, while the iron is hot – fly, sir, begone –

SMITH

What! What would you have me do, doctor? I wish the stars   55
would put me in a way for this fine place.

KITE

The stars do – let me see – aye, about an hour hence walk
carelessly into the market-place and you'll see a tall, slender
gentleman cheapening a pen'worth of apples, with a cane
hanging upon his button – this gentleman will ask you what's   60
o'clock – he's your man, and the maker of your fortune;
follow him, follow him. And now go home and take leave of
your wife and children; an hour hence exactly is your time.

SMITH

A tall, slender gentleman, you say! With a cane. Pray, what
sort of a head has the cane?   65

KITE

An amber head with a black ribband.

SMITH

But pray, of what employment is the gentleman?

KITE

Let me see – he's either a collector of the excise, or a pleni-
potentiary, or a captain of grenadiers – I can't tell exactly
which. But he'll call you honest – your name is –   70

SMITH

Thomas.

49 *Sir . . . 'em* Q2 (So am I sir Q1)
59 *cheapening* bargaining for   68 *excise, or a* Q2 (excise, a Q1)

50–1 *Captain of the Forges* Dixon notes this is an invented title.
52 *two servants* See Appendix 5.
65 f. N.T.: 'Plume, who is hidden behind a screen, brandishes his cane in
front of Kite's face' (Tynan).

KITE

He'll call you honest Tom.

SMITH

But how the devil should he know my name?

KITE

Oh, there are several sorts of Toms – Tom a'Lincoln, Tom-
tit, Tom Telltroth, Tom o'Bedlam, Tom Fool. – (*Knocking*   75
at the door) Begone – an hour hence precisely.

SMITH

You say he'll ask me what's o'clock?

KITE

Most certainly, and you'll answer you don't know, and be
sure you look at St Mary's dial, for the sun won't shine, and
if it should, you won't be able to tell the figures.   80

SMITH

I will, I will.   *Exit*

PLUME ([*Appearing*] *behind*)

Well done, conjurer, go on and prosper.

KITE

As you were.

Enter [PLUCK] *a* BUTCHER

KITE (*Aside*)

What, my old friend Pluck the butcher – I offered the surly
bulldog five guineas this morning and he refused it.   85

BUTCHER

So, Master Conjurer, here's half a crown – and now you
must understand –

KITE

Hold, friend, I know your business beforehand.

72 *He'll* Q2 (Right, he'll Q1)   74 *Tom-tit* blue titmouse
75 *Tom Telltroth* honest man
  Tom o' Bedlam released lunatic, licensed to beg; also, type of
  beggar who pretended madness
  Tom Fool (a) half wit (b) buffoon
83 s.d. PLUCK heart, liver, lungs, etc. of a beast, used as food

74 *Tom a' Lincoln*. 'The Red Rose Knight', protagonist of Richard Johnson's
romance, *The Most Pleasant History of Tom a Lincolne* (Stationers'
Register, 2 pt., 1599, 1607), of which a new edition appeared in
1705, and also of an unpublished tragi-comedy attributed to Thomas
Heywood. There was a 'famous bear' of the same name (see William
Cavendish, *The Humorous Lovers*, [1677], p. 48), and a large bell in
Lincoln Cathedral.

BUTCHER

You're devilish cunning then; for I don't well know it myself.

KITE

I know more than you, friend – you have a foolish saying,   90
that such a one knows no more than the man in the moon;
I tell you the man in the moon knows more than all the men
under the sun; don't the moon see all the world?

BUTCHER

All the world see the moon, I must confess.

KITE

Then she must see all the world, that's certain. Give me   95
your hand – you're by trade either a butcher or a surgeon.

BUTCHER

True, I am a butcher.

KITE

And a surgeon you will be, the employments differ only in
the name – he that can cut up an ox, may dissect a man, and
the same dexterity that cracks a marrow-bone will cut off a   100
leg or an arm.

BUTCHER

What d'ye mean, doctor, what d'ye mean?

KITE

Patience, patience, Mr Surgeon-General, the stars are great
bodies and move slowly.

BUTCHER

But what d'ye mean by Surgeon-General, doctor?   105

KITE

Nay, sir, if your worship won't have patience, I must beg the
favour of your worship's absence.

BUTCHER

My worship, my worship! But why my worship?

KITE

Nay, then I have done.   *Sits*

BUTCHER

Pray, doctor.   110

KITE

Fire and fury, sir! (*Rises in a passion*) Do you think the stars
will be hurried? Do the stars owe you any money, sir, that
you dare to dun their lordships at this rate? Sir, I am porter
to the stars, and I am ordered to let no dun come near their
doors.   115

---

91 *the man in the moon* proverbial. Tilley, M240
96 *you're* Q2 (you are Q1)   103 *Surgeon-General* See Appendix 5.

BUTCHER

Dear doctor, I never had any dealings with the stars, they don't owe me a penny – but since you are their porter, please to accept of this half-crown to drink their healths, and don't be angry.

KITE

Let me see your hand then once more – here has been gold – 120
five guineas, my friend, in this very hand this morning.

BUTCHER

Nay, then he is the devil – pray, doctor, were you born of a woman, or did you come into the world of your own head?

KITE

That's a secret – this gold was offered you by a proper, hand-some man, called Hawk, or Buzzard, or – 125

BUTCHER

Kite, you mean.

KITE

Aye, aye, Kite.

BUTCHER

As errant a rogue as ever carried a halberd – the impudent rascal would have decoyed me for a soldier.

KITE

A soldier! A man of your substance for a soldier! Your 130
mother has a hundred pound in hard money lying at this minute in the hands of a mercer, not forty yards from this place.

BUTCHER

Oons, and so she has, but very few know so much.

KITE

I know it, and that rogue, what's his name, Kite, knew it, and 135
offered you five guineas to list because he knew your poor mother would give the hundred for your discharge.

BUTCHER

There's a dog now – flesh, doctor, I'll give you t'other half-crown, and tell me that this same Kite will be hanged.

KITE

He's in as much danger as any man in the county of Salop. 140

BUTCHER

There's your fee – but you have forgot the Surgeon-General all this while.

KITE

You put the stars in a passion.   *Looks on his books*

117 *their porter* Q2 (the porter Q1)

But now they're pacified again – let me see – did you never
cut off a man's leg?   145

BUTCHER

No.

KITE

Recollect, pray.

BUTCHER

I say no.

KITE

That's strange, wonderful strange; but nothing is strange to
me, such wonderful changes have I seen – the second or   150
third, aye, the third campaign that you make in Flanders, the
leg of a great officer will be shattered by a great shot; you will
be there accidentally, and with your cleaver chop off the limb
at a blow; in short, the operation will be performed with so
much dexterity, that with general applause you will be made   155
Surgeon-General of the whole army.

BUTCHER

Nay, for the matter of cutting off a limb, I'll do't, I'll do't
with any surgeon in Europe, but I have no thoughts of
making a campaign.

KITE

You have no thoughts! What matter for your thoughts? The   160
stars have decreed it, and you must go.

BUTCHER

The stars decree it! Oons, sir, the justices can't press me.

KITE

Nay, friend, 'tis none of my business, I ha' done. Only mind
this, you'll know more an hour and a half hence – that's all –
farewell.   *Going*   165

BUTCHER

Hold, hold, doctor, Surgeon-General! What is the place
worth, pray?

KITE

Five hundred pound a year, beside guineas for claps.

BUTCHER

Five hundred pound a year! – An hour and half hence you
say?   170

KITE

Prithee, friend, be quiet, don't be so troublesome, here's

---

155 *general* Q2 (the general Q1)
166 *What* Q2 (Pray what Q1)
168 *for claps* i.e., for curing gonorrhoea

such a work to make a booby butcher accept of five hundred
pound a year. – But if you must hear it – I tell you in short,
you'll be standing in your stall an hour and half hence, and
a gentleman will come by with a snuff-box in his hand, and   175
the tip of his handkerchief hanging out of his right pocket;
he'll ask you the price of a loin of veal, and at the same time
stroke your great dog upon the head and call him Chopper.

BUTCHER

Mercy upon us! Chopper is the dog's name.

KITE

Look'ee there – what I say is true, things that are to come   180
must come to pass. Get you home, sell off your stock, don't
mind the whining and the snivelling of your mother and
your sister, women always hinder preferment; make what
money you can and follow that gentleman, his name begins
with a P – mind that. There will be the barber's daughter,   185
too, that you promised marriage to, she will be pulling and
hauling you to pieces.

BUTCHER

What! Know Sally too? He's the devil, and he needs must
go that the devil drives. – (*Going*) The tip of his handkerchief
out of his left pocket?   190

KITE

No, no, his right pocket; if it be the left, 'tis none of the man.

BUTCHER

Well, well, I'll mind him.   *Exit*

PLUME (*Behind with his pocket-book*)

The right pocket, you say?

KITE

I hear the rustling of silks. (*Knocking*) Fly, sir, 'tis Madam
Melinda.   195

Enter MELINDA *and* LUCY

KITE [*To* SERVANT]

Tycho, chairs for the ladies.

MELINDA

Don't trouble yourself, we shan't stay, doctor.

KITE

Your ladyship is to stay much longer than you imagine.

187 *hauling* Q2 (haleing Q1)
188–9 *he needs . . . drives* proverbial. Tilley, D278

MELINDA

For what?

KITE

For a husband. – (*To* LUCY) For your part, madam, you   200
won't stay for a husband.

LUCY

Pray, doctor, do you converse with the stars, or with the
devil?

KITE

With both; when I have the destinies of men in search, I
consult the stars; when the affairs of women come under my   205
hand, I advise with my t'other friend.

MELINDA

And have you raised the devil upon my account?

KITE

Yes, madam, and he's now under the table.

LUCY

Oh, heavens protect us! Dear madam, let us be gone.

KITE

If you be afraid of him, why do you come to consult him?   210

MELINDA

Don't fear, fool. Do you think, sir, that because I'm a woman
I'm to be fooled out of my reason, or frighted out of my
senses? – Come, show me this devil.

KITE

He's a little busy at present, but when he has done he shall
wait on you.   215

MELINDA

What is he doing?

KITE

Writing your name in his pocket-book.

MELINDA

Ha, ha, ha, my name! Pray, what have you or he to do with
my name?

KITE

Look'ee, fair lady – the devil is a very modest person, he seeks   220
nobody unless they seek him first; he's chained up like a
mastiff, and can't stir unless he be let loose. – You come to
me to have your fortune told – do you think, madam, that I
can answer you of my own head? No, madam, the affairs of
women are so irregular, that nothing less than the devil can   225
give any account of 'em. Now to convince you of your
incredulity, I'll show you a trial of my skill. – Here, you

Cacodemon\del fuego, exert your power,–draw me this lady's
name, the word Melinda, in the proper letters and character
of her own handwriting. – Do it at three motions – one –   230
two – three – 'tis done – now, madam, will you please to send
your maid to fetch it.

LUCY

I fetch it! The devil fetch me if I do.

MELINDA

My name in my own handwriting! That would be convincing
indeed.   235

KITE

Seeing's believing.   *Goes to the table, lifts up the carpet*
Here Tre, Tre, poor Tre, give me the bone, sirrah. – There's
your name upon that square piece of paper – behold –

MELINDA

'Tis wonderful! My very letters to a tittle.

LUCY

'Tis like your hand, madam, but not so like your hand   240
neither, and now I look nearer, 'tis not like your hand at all.

KITE

Here's a chambermaid now will out-lie the devil.

LUCY

Look'ee, madam, they shan't impose upon us; people can't
remember their hands no more than they can their faces. –

---

228 *Cacodemon del fuego* Q1 (*Cacodemon del Plumo* Q2)
237 *Tre* pronounced 'Tray', common C18 dog's name
    sirrah.—There's Q2 (11 lines of additional text Q1) see Appendix
    1, A, iii, a
242 *now will* Q2 (now that will Q1)

---

228 *Cacodemon del fuego*. Q1's reading, evil spirit from hell, makes ready
    sense, 'while the use of Plume's name is incautious and out of character'
    (Strauss). It is not needed in Q2 to cue him to be ready to hand over the
    paper; still, it must have come from the theatre, and received Farquhar's
    sanction.
237 *sirrah*. There follows in Q1 the passage in which Plume grabs Kite's
    hand under the table, and makes him believe for a moment that this is
    'the devil in good earnest!' Archer in describing it as an 'outrageously
    farcical passage, which was doubtless found ineffective, and therefore
    omitted in Q2,' is probably right. It seems awkward to stage, without
    the girls catching sight of Plume. As its presence significantly alters the
    effect of the scene towards farce the present edition follows Q2: it, and
    the related passage following l.280 below, have been relegated to
    Appendix 1.

Come, madam, let us be certain, write your name upon this   245
paper, then we'll compare the two names.

Takes out paper and folds it

KITE

Anything for your satisfaction, madam – here's pen and ink.

MELINDA *writes*, LUCY *holds the paper*

LUCY

Let me see it, madam, 'tis the same, the very same. – (*Aside*)
But I'll secure one copy for my own affairs.

MELINDA

This is demonstration.   250

KITE

'Tis so, madam, the word 'demonstration' comes from
Daemon the father of lies.

MELINDA

Well, doctor, I'm convinced; and now pray what account
can you give me of my future fortune?

KITE

Before the sun has made one course round this earthly globe,   255
your fortune will be fixed for happiness or misery.

MELINDA

What! So near the crisis of my fate!

KITE

Let me see – about the hour of ten tomorrow morning you
will be saluted by a gentleman who will come to take his leave
of you, being designed for travel. His intention of going   260
abroad is sudden, and the occasion a woman. Your fortune
and his are like the bullet and the barrel, one runs plump
into the t'other. – In short, if the gentleman travels he will
die abroad, and if he does you will die before he comes home.

MELINDA

What sort of man is he?   265

KITE

Madam, he's a fine gentleman, and a lover – that is, a man of
very good sense, and a very great fool.

MELINDA

How is that possible, doctor?

KITE

Because, madam – because it is so: a woman's reason is the
best for a man's being a fool.   270

247 s.d. LUCY Q2 (*and* LUCY Q1)
262 *plump* directly (muzzle loaded)
266 *he's* Q2 (he is Q1)
269 *a woman's reason* it is so because it is so

MELINDA

Ten o'clock, you say?

KITE

Ten, about the hour of tea-drinking throughout the kingdom.

MELINDA

Here, doctor. (*Gives money*) Lucy, have you any questions
to ask?

LUCY

Oh, madam! a thousand. 275

KITE

I must beg your patience till another time, for I expect more
company this minute; besides, I must discharge the gentleman under the table.

LUCY

Oh, pray, sir, discharge us first.

KITE

Tycho, wait on the ladies downstairs. 280

Exit MELINDA *and* LUCY

Enter PLUME *and* WORTHY

KITE

Mr Worthy, you were pleased to wish me joy today, I hope
to be able to return the compliment tomorrow.

WORTHY

I'll make it the best compliment to you that ever I made in
my life, if you do; but I must be a traveller, you say?

KITE

No farther than the chops of the Channel, I presume, sir. 285

PLUME

That we have concerted already. (*Knocking hard*) Hey day!
You don't profess midwifery, doctor?

KITE

Away to your ambuscade. *Exeunt* PLUME *and* WORTHY

273 s.d. *Gives money* Q2 (*Gives him money* Q1)
279 *Oh* Q2 (not in Q1)
279 f. so, Q2 (7 lines of additional text Q1) see Appendix 1, A, iii, b
283–4 *ever I made in my* Q2 (you ever made in your Q1)
   compliment pun on sense 'complimentary gift'
285 *chops* entrance to the English channel, approached from the
   Atlantic

272 *tea-drinking* Tea was expensive (16*s* to 18*s* a pound in 1706) and the
   tea-table an established female institution (see Ashton, pp. 73, 154;
   Congreve, *The Way of the World*, IV.v, 129f.).

Enter BRAZEN

BRAZEN
　Your servant, servant, my dear.

KITE
　Stand off, I have my familiar already.　　　　　290

BRAZEN
　Are you bewitched, my dear?

KITE
　Yes, my dear, but mine is a peaceable spirit, and hates
　gunpowder – thus I fortify myself; (*draws a circle round
　him*) and now, Captain, have a care how you force my lines.

BRAZEN
　Lines! What dost talk of lines? You have something like a　295
　fishing-rod there, indeed; but I come to be acquainted
　with you, man – what's your name, my dear?

KITE
　Conundrum.

BRAZEN
　Conundrum! Rat me, I know a famous doctor in London of
　your name – where were you born?　　　　　300

KITE
　I was born in Algebra.

BRAZEN
　Algebra! – 'Tis no country in Christendom I'm sure,
　unless it be some pitiful place in the Highlands of Scotland.

KITE
　Right! I told you I was bewitched.

BRAZEN
　So am I, my dear, I'm going to be married – I've had two　305
　letters from a lady of fortune that loves me to madness, fits,
　colic, spleen, and vapours – shall I marry her in four and
　twenty hours, aye or no?

KITE
　I must have the year and day o'th' month when these
　letters were dated.　　　　　310

BRAZEN
　Why, you old bitch, did you ever hear of love-letters dated
　with the year and day o'th' month? Do you think *billets doux*
　are like bank bills?

KITE
　They are not so good – but if they bear no date, I must
　examine the contents.　　　　　315

BRAZEN

Contents, that you shall, old boy, [*pulls out two letters*] here
they be both.

KITE

Only the last you received, if you please. (*Takes the letter*)
Now, sir, if you please to let me consult my books for a
minute, I'll send this letter enclosed to you with the deter-   320
mination of the stars upon it to your lodgings.

BRAZEN

With all my heart – I must give him – (*puts his hand in his
pocket*) Algebra! I fancy, doctor, 'tis hard to calculate the
place of your nativity – here. – (*Gives him money*) And if I
succeed, I'll build a watchtower upon the top of the highest   325
mountain in Wales for the study of astrology, and the benefit of Conundrums.   *Exit*

Enter PLUME *and* WORTHY

WORTHY

Oh! Doctor, that letter's worth a million, let me see it –
and now I have it, I'm afraid to open it.

PLUME

Pho, let me see it! (*Opening the letter*) If she be a jilt – damn   330
her, she is one – there's her name at the bottom on't.

WORTHY

How! – Then I'll travel in good earnest – by all my hopes,
'tis Lucy's hand.

PLUME

Lucy's!

WORTHY

Certainly, 'tis no more like Melinda's character than black   335
is to white.

PLUME

Then 'tis certainly Lucy's contrivance to draw in Brazen
for a husband – but are you sure 'tis not Melinda's hand?

WORTHY

You shall see; where's the bit of paper I gave you just now
that the devil writ 'Melinda' upon?   340

KITE

Here, sir.

PLUME

'Tis plain, they're not the same; and is this the malicious

322 s.d. *in his* Q2 (*in's* Q1)
332 *I'll* Q2 (I will Q1)

name that was subscribed to the letter which made Mr
Balance send his daughter into the country?

WORTHY

The very same, the other fragments I showed you just now.   345

PLUME

But 'twas barbarous to conceal this so long, and to continue me so many hours in the pernicious heresy of believing
that angelic creature could change – poor Silvia!

WORTHY

Rich Silvia, you mean, and poor captain – ha, ha, ha; come,
come, friend, Melinda is true and shall be mine; Silvia is   350
constant and may be yours.

PLUME

No, she's above my hopes – but for her sake I'll recant my
opinion of her sex.

By some the sex is blamed without design,
Light, harmless censure, such as yours and mine,   355
Sallies of wit, and vapours of our wine.
Others the justice of the sex condemn,
And wanting merit to create esteem,
Would hide their own defects by cens'ring them.
But they, secure in their all-conqu'ring charms,   360
Laugh at the vain efforts of false alarms;
He magnifies their conquests who complains,
For none would struggle were they not in chains.

Exeunt

Act V, Scene i

An Antechamber [adjoining SILVIA's *bedroom], with a
periwig, hat, and sword upon the table
Enter* SILVIA *in her nightcap*

SILVIA

I have rested but indifferently, and I believe my bedfellow
was as little pleased; poor Rose! Here she comes –

Enter ROSE

Good morrow, my dear, how d'ye this morning?

345 *now* Q2 (now, I once intended it for another use, but I think I
        have turned it now to better advantage Q1)
361 *false alarms* (presumably) false attacks, feints
363 s.d. *Exeunt* Q2 (not in Q1)
        Scene i wholly omitted in Q2

ROSE

Just as I was last night, neither better nor worse for you.

SILVIA

What's the matter? Did you not like your bedfellow?   5

ROSE

I don't know whether I had a bedfellow or not.

SILVIA

Did not I lie with you?

ROSE

No – I wonder you could have the conscience to ruin a poor
girl for nothing.

SILVIA

I have saved thee from ruin, child; don't be melancholy, I   10
can give you as many fine things as the captain can.

ROSE

But you can't, I'm sure.   *Knocking at the door*

SILVIA

Odso! My accoutrements – (*Puts on her periwig, hat, and
sword*) Who's at the door?

[MOB] (*Without*)

Open the door, or we'll break it down.   15

SILVIA

Patience a little –   *Opens the door*

        Enter [MR BRIDEWELL, *a*] CONSTABLE *and* WATCH

CONSTABLE

We have 'em, we have 'em, the duck and the mallard both
in the decoy.

SILVIA

What means this riot? Stand off! (*Draws*) The man dies
that comes within reach of my point.   20

CONSTABLE

That is not the point, master, put up your sword or I shall
knock you down; and so I command the Queen's peace.

SILVIA

You are some blockhead of a constable.

CONSTABLE

I am so, and have a warrant to apprehend the bodies of you
and your whore there.   25

15 s.p. [MOB] *Dixon* (not in Qq)
16 s.d. WATCH Ed. (MOB Q1)   17 *mallard* male of wild duck
22 *command . . . peace* command you to keep the peace (rendering
     further resistance a breach of it)

ROSE

Whore! Never was poor woman so abused.

Enter BULLOCK *unbuttoned*

BULLOCK

What's matter now? – Oh! Mr Bridewell, what brings you
abroad so early?

CONSTABLE

This, sir – (*Lays hold of* BULLOCK) You're the Queen's
prisoner.   30

BULLOCK

Wauns, you lie, sir, I'm the Queen's soldier.

CONSTABLE

No matter for that, you shall go before Justice Balance.

SILVIA

Balance! 'Tis what I wanted. – Here, Mr Constable, I
resign my sword.

ROSE

Can't you carry us before the captain, Mr Bridewell?   35

CONSTABLE

Captain! Han't you got your bellyful of captains yet? Come,
come, make way there.   *Exeunt*

[Act V], Scene ii

JUSTICE BALANCE'*s house*
Enter BALANCE *and* SCALE

SCALE

I say 'tis not to be borne, Mr Balance.

BALANCE

Look'ee, Mr Scale, for my own part I shall be very tender
in what regards the officers of the army; they expose their
lives to so many dangers for us abroad that we may give
them some grains of allowance at home.   5

SCALE

Allowance! This poor girl's father is my tenant, and if I
mistake not, her mother nursed a child for you; shall they
debauch our daughters to our faces?

BALANCE

Consider, Mr Scale, that were it not for the bravery of these

27 *Bridewell* ex. house of correction
0.1 s.d. *Enter* Q2 (not in Q1)

officers we should have French dragoons among us, that   10
would leave us neither liberty, property, wife, nor daughter. – Come, Mr Scale, the gentlemen are vigorous and
warm, and may they continue so; the same heat that stirs
them up to love, spurs them on to battle; you never knew a
great general in your life that did not love a whore. This I   15
only speak in reference to Captain Plume, for the other spark
I know nothing of.

SCALE

Nor can I hear of anybody that does – oh, here they come.
     Enter SILVIA, BULLOCK, ROSE, *prisoners*; CONSTABLE *and*
                    WATCH

CONSTABLE

May it please your worships, we took them in the very act,
re infecta, sir – the gentleman indeed behaved himself like   20
a gentleman, for he drew his sword and swore, and afterwards laid it down and said nothing.

BALANCE

Give the gentleman his sword again – wait you without.
               Exeunt CONSTABLE *and* WATCH
(*To* SILVIA) I'm sorry, sir, to know a gentleman upon such
terms, that the occasion of our meeting should prevent the   25
satisfaction of an acquaintance.

SILVIA

Sir, you need make no apology for your warrant, no more
than I shall do for my behaviour – my innocence is upon an
equal foot with your authority.

SCALE

Innocence! Have you not seduced that young maid?   30

SILVIA

No, Mr Goosecap, she seduced me.

BULLOCK

So she did, I'll swear – for she proposed marriage first.

BALANCE

What! Then you're married, child?   (*To* ROSE)

20 *re infecta* the act not having been accomplished
23 s.d. *and* WATCH Q2 (*&c.* Q1)
25 *prevent* anticipate
31 *Goosecap* alluding to his Justice's wig; dolt

---

10 *French dragoons* Englishmen generally were convinced that, subjected
to Louis XIV, they would have lawless dragoons forcibly quartered on
them, as had happened to the French Huguenots since the Revocation
of the Edict of Nantes in 1685, to harry them into conversion to Cath-
olicism.

ROSE

Yes, sir, to my sorrow.

BALANCE

Who was witness?   35

BULLOCK

That was I – I danced, threw the stocking, and spoke jokes
by their bedside, I'm sure.

BALANCE

Who was the minister?

BULLOCK

Minister! We are soldiers, and want no ministers – they
were married by the Articles of War.   40

BALANCE

Hold thy prating, fool. Your appearance, sir, promises
some understanding; pray, what does this fellow mean?

SILVIA

He means marriage, I think – but that, you know, is so odd
a thing, that hardly any two people under the sun agree in
the ceremony; some make it a sacrament, others a con-   45
venience, and others make it a jest; but among soldiers
'tis most sacred – our sword, you know, is our honour; that
we lay down, the hero jumps over it first, and the amazon
after – leap rogue, follow whore – the drum beats a ruff,
and so to bed; that's all, the ceremony is concise.   50

BULLOCK

And the prettiest ceremony, so full of pastime and prod-
igality –

BALANCE

What! Are you a soldier?

BULLOCK

Aye, that I am. Will your worship lend me your cane, and
I'll show you how I can exercise.   55

38 *minister* Q2 (ministers Q1)

---

36 *threw the stocking*. Part of the knockabout fun traditional for weddings:
when the newly-weds are in bed,

> The bridesmen take the bride's stockings, and the bridesmaids the
> bridegroom's; both sit down at the bed's feet and fling the stockings
> over their heads, endeavouring to direct them so as that they may fall
> upon the married couple. If the man's stockings, thrown by the maids,
> fall upon the bridegroom's head, it is a sign she will quickly be married
> herself; and the same prognostic holds good of the woman's stockings
> thrown by the man.

(*M. Misson's Memoirs*, etc., translated by Ozells (1719); cited from
Ashton, p. 33).

BALANCE

Take it. (*Strikes him over the head*) Pray, sir, what commission may you bear?   (*To* SILVIA)

SILVIA

I'm called Captain, sir, by all the coffeemen, drawers, whores, and groom-porters in London, for I wear a red coat, a sword, a hat *bien troussé*, a martial twist in my cravat,   60
a fierce knot in my periwig, a cane upon my button, piquet in my head, and dice in my pocket.

SCALE

Your name, pray, sir?

SILVIA

Captain Pinch; I cock my hat with a pinch, I take snuff with a pinch, pay my whores with a pinch; in short, I can   65
do anything at a pinch, but fight and fill my belly.

BALANCE

And pray, sir, what brought you into Shropshire?

SILVIA

A pinch, sir: I knew you country gentlemen want wit, and you know that we town gentlemen want money, and so –

BALANCE

I understand you, sir. – Here, Constable!   70

Enter CONSTABLE

Take this gentleman into custody till farther orders.

ROSE

Pray your worship, don't be uncivil to him, for he did me no hurt; he's the most harmless man in the world, for all he talks so.

SCALE

Come, come, child, I'll take care of you.   75

SILVIA

What, gentlemen, rob me of my freedom and my wife at once! 'Tis the first time they ever went together.

BALANCE (*Whispers*)

Hark'ee, Constable –

---

58 *coffeemen* coffee-house keepers *drawers* tapsters
59 *groom-porters* royal officers appointed to supervise gaming
60 *a hat* Q2 (not in Q1)
    bien troussé neatly arranged
61 *piquet* card-game
68 *knew you* Q2 (knew that you Q1)
78 s.d. *Whispers* Ed. (*Whispers the Constable* Q)

CONSTABLE

It shall be done, sir. – Come along, sir.

Exeunt CONSTABLE, BULLOCK *and* SILVIA

BALANCE

Come, Mr Scale, we'll manage the spark presently.   80

Exeunt BALANCE, [ROSE] *and* SCALE

[Act V], Scene iii

MELINDA'S *Apartment*
Enter MELINDA *and* WORTHY

MELINDA

(*Aside*) So far the prediction is right, 'tis ten exactly. –
And pray sir, how long have you been in this travelling
humour?

WORTHY

'Tis natural, madam, for us to avoid what disturbs our quiet.

MELINDA

Rather the love of change, which is more natural, may be the   5
occasion of it.

WORTHY

To be sure, madam, there must be charms in variety, else
neither you nor I should be so fond of it.

MELINDA

You mistake, Mr Worthy, I am not so fond of variety as to
travel for't, nor do I think it prudence in you to run your-   10
self into a certain expense and danger, in hopes of precarious pleasures which at best never answer expectation,
as 'tis evident from the example of most travellers, that
long more to return to their own country than they did to
go abroad.   15

WORTHY

What pleasures I may receive abroad are indeed uncertain;
but this I am sure of, I shall meet with less cruelty among
the most barbarous nations than I have found at home.

MELINDA

Come, sir, you and I have been jangling a great while; I
fancy if we made up our accounts, we should the sooner   20
come to an agreement.

WORTHY

Sure, madam, you won't dispute your being in my debt –

0.2 s.d. MELINDA'S *Apartment* Q2 ([SCENE] *changes to* MELINDA'S
     Apartment Q1)
0.1 s.d. *Enter* Q2 (not in Q1)   10 *for't* Q2 (for it Q1)

my fears, sighs, vows, promises, assiduities, anxieties,
jealousies, have run on for a whole year, without any pay-
ment.   25

MELINDA

A year! Oh Mr Worthy, what you owe to me is not to be
paid under a seven years' servitude. How did you use me the
year before, when taking the advantage of my innocence and
necessity, you would have made me your mistress, that is,
your slave? Remember the wicked insinuations, artful baits,   30
deceitful arguments, cunning pretences; then your impudent behaviour, loose expressions, familiar letters, rude
visits; remember those, those, Mr Worthy.

WORTHY

(*Aside*) I do remember, and am sorry I made no better use
of 'em. – But you may remember, madam, that –   35

MELINDA

Sir, I'll remember nothing – 'tis your interest that I should
forget; you have been barbarous to me, I have been cruel to
you; put that and that together, and let one balance the
other. Now if you will begin upon a new score, lay aside
your adventuring airs, and behave yourself handsomely till   40
Lent be over, here's my hand, I'll use you as a gentleman
should be.

WORTHY

And if I don't use you as a gentlewoman should be, may
this be my poison.   *Kissing her hand*

Enter SERVANT

SERVANT

Madam, the coach is at the door.   45

MELINDA

I'm going to Mr Balance's country-house to see my cousin
Silvia; I have done her an injury, and can't be easy till I have
asked her pardon.

WORTHY

I dare not hope for the honour of waiting on you.

MELINDA

My coach is full, but if you will be so gallant as to mount   50

27 *seven years' servitude* cf. *Genesis* 29:18–30
41 *Lent* meant figuratively

---

50 *My coach is full.* Separation of Melinda and Worthy is essential for the
    subsequent complication, yet its justification is slapdash: 'Lucy,
    presumably, is to be Melinda's companion, yet this arrangement clashes
    with Lucy's plan concerning Brazen' (Strauss).

your own horses and follow us, we shall be glad to be
overtaken; and if you bring Captain Plume with you, we
shan't have the worse reception.

WORTHY

I'll endeavour it.   *Exit* WORTHY *leading* MELINDA

[Act V], Scene iv
The Market-place
Enter PLUME *and* KITE

PLUME

A baker, a tailor, a smith, and a butcher – I believe the first
colony planted at Virginia had not more trades in their
company than I have in mine.

KITE

The butcher, sir, will have his hands full; for we have two
sheep stealers among us – I hear of a fellow, too, com-   5
mitted just now for stealing of horses.

PLUME

We'll dispose of him among the dragoons. Have we ne'er a
poulterer among us?

KITE

Yes, sir, the king of the gypsies is a very good one, he has an
excellent hand at a goose or a turkey. Here's Captain Brazen,   10
sir – I must go look after the men.   *Exit*

Enter BRAZEN *reading a letter*

BRAZEN

Um, um, um, the canonical hour – um, um, very well. – My
dear Plume! Give me a buss.

PLUME

Half a score if you will, my dear. [*They kiss*] What hast got
in thy hand, child?   15

BRAZEN

'Tis a project for laying out a thousand pound.

PLUME

Were it not requisite to project first how to get it in?

1–2 *first . . . Virginia*. Established at Jamestown, 1607.
5–6 *sheep stealers . . . horses*. Under the Impressment and Mutiny Acts,
    convicted felons could avoid civil punishment by enlisting.

BRAZEN

You can't imagine, my dear, that I want a thousand pound;
I have spent twenty times as much in the service – now, my
dear, pray advise me, my head runs much upon architec-   20
ture; shall I build a privateer or a playhouse?

PLUME

An odd question – a privateer or a playhouse! 'Twill require
some consideration. – Faith, I'm for a privateer.

BRAZEN

I'm not of your opinion, my dear – for in the first place a
privateer may be ill-built.   25

PLUME

And so may a playhouse.

BRAZEN

But a privateer may be ill-manned.

PLUME

And so may a playhouse.

BRAZEN

But a privateer may run upon the shallows.

PLUME

Not so often as a playhouse.   30

BRAZEN

But, you know, a privateer may spring a leak.

PLUME

And I know that a playhouse may spring a great many.

BRAZEN

But suppose the privateer come home with a rich booty, we
should never agree about our shares.

PLUME

'Tis just so in a playhouse – so by my advice, you shall fix   35
upon the privateer.

---

18 *a thousand* Ed. (twenty thousand Q)

18 *thousand.* Q1's 'twenty' is clearly caught from the line below; for if
   Brazen said 'twenty thousand' here Plume would not react so sharply
   when he says it at l.37. Even Brazen would scarcely boast of spending
   twenty times this.
20–36 This reflects upon the current problems of the two rival theatres,
   and primarily on those of the Queen's Theatre in the Haymarket,
   opened in April 1705. Sir John Vanbrugh had raised the capital by
   subscription to build a handsome theatre, yet its acoustics were very
   poor, Betterton's acting-company had few good actors left, and the first
   year's productions usually flopped (see *An Apology for the Life of Colley
   Cibber*, op. cit., ch. IX; *The London Stage, Part II*, introduction).

BRAZEN

Agreed – but if this twenty thousand should not be in specie –

PLUME

What twenty thousand?

BRAZEN

Hark'ee –   *Whispers*   40

PLUME

Married!

BRAZEN

Presently, we're to meet about half a mile out of town at the waterside – and so forth – (*Reads*) 'For fear I should be known by any of Worthy's friends, you must give me leave to wear my mask till after the ceremony, which will make me   45
ever yours'. – Look'ee there, my dear dog –
                    Shows the bottom of the letter to PLUME

PLUME

Melinda! And by this light, her own hand! – Once more, if you please, my dear; her hand exactly! – Just now you say?

BRAZEN

This minute I must be gone.

PLUME

Have a little patience, and I'll go with you.   50

BRAZEN

No, no, I see a gentleman coming this way that may be inquisitive; 'tis Worthy, do you know him?

PLUME

By sight only.

BRAZEN

Have a care, the very eyes discover secrets –   *Exit*

Enter WORTHY

WORTHY

To boot and saddle, Captain, you must mount.   55

PLUME

Whip and spur, Worthy, or you won't mount.

WORTHY

But I shall: Melinda and I are agreed; she's gone to visit Silvia, we are to mount and follow, and could we carry a parson with us, who knows what might be done for us both?

PLUME

Don't trouble your head, Melinda has secured a parson   60
already.

38 *specie* coin, ready money   57 *she's* Q2 (she is Q1)

WORTHY
Already! Do you know more than I?

PLUME
Yes, I saw it under her hand – Brazen and she are to meet
half a mile hence at the waterside, there to take boat, I suppose to be ferried over to the Elysian fields, if there be any   65
such thing in matrimony.

WORTHY
I parted with Melinda just now; she assured me she hated
Brazen, and that she resolved to discard Lucy for daring to
write letters to him in her name.

PLUME
Nay, nay, there's nothing of Lucy in this – I tell ye I saw   70
Melinda's hand as surely as this is mine.

WORTHY
But I tell you, she's gone this minute to Justice Balance's
country-house.

PLUME
But I tell you, she's gone this minute to the waterside.

Enter a SERVANT

SERVANT (*to* WORTHY)
Madam Melinda has sent word that you need not trouble   75
yourself to follow her, because her journey to Justice
Balance's is put off, and she's gone to take the air another
way.

WORTHY
How! Her journey put off?

PLUME
That is, her journey was a put-off to you.   80

WORTHY
'Tis plain, plain – but how, where, when is she to meet
Brazen?

PLUME
Just now, I tell you, half a mile hence at the waterside.

WORTHY
Up, or down the water?

PLUME
That I don't know.   85

WORTHY
I'm glad my horses are ready. – Jack, get 'em out.
                                    [*Exit* SERVANT]

PLUME
Shall I go with you?

WORTHY

Not an inch; I shall return presently.

PLUME

You'll find me at the hall; the justices are sitting by this
time, and I must attend them.   [*Exeunt severally*]   90

[Act V], Scene v

A Court of Justice
BALANCE, SCALE *and* SCRUPLE *upon the bench;*
CONSTABLE, KITE, *Mob* [*in attendance*]
KITE *and* CONSTABLE *advance forward*

KITE

Pray, who are those honourable gentlemen upon the bench?

CONSTABLE

He in the middle is Justice Balance, he on the right is
Justice Scale, and he on the left is Justice Scruple, and I
am Mr Constable, four very honest gentlemen.

KITE

Oh dear sir, I'm your most obedient servant. (*Saluting the*   5
CONSTABLE) I fancy, sir, that your employment and mine are
much the same, for my business is to keep people in order,
and if they disobey, to knock 'em down; and then we're
both staff-officers.

CONSTABLE

Nay, I'm a sergeant myself – of the militia. Come, brother,   10
you shall see me exercise – suppose this a musket now.
(*He puts his staff on his right shoulder*) Now I'm shouldered.

KITE

Aye, you're shouldered pretty well for a constable's staff,
but for a musket you must put it on t'other shoulder, my
dear.   15

CONSTABLE

Adso! That's true. – Come, now give the word o'command.

KITE

Silence.

CONSTABLE

Aye, aye, so we will, – we will be silent.

90 *Exeunt severally* Ed. (88, 90 *Exit* Qq)
 0.3 s.d. *and* Q2 (not in Q1)
 0.1 s.d. *forward* Q2 (*to the front of the stage* Q1)

KITE

Silence, you dog, silence –

Strikes him over the head with his halberd

CONSTABLE

That's the way to silence a man with a witness! – What d'ye   20
mean, friend?

KITE

Only to exercise you, sir.

CONSTABLE

Your exercise differs so from ours, that we shall ne'er agree
about it; if my own captain had given me such a rap, I had
taken the law of him.   25

Enter PLUME

BALANCE

Captain, you're welcome.

PLUME

Gentlemen, I thank'ee.

SCRUPLE

Come, honest Captain, sit by me. (PLUME *ascends, and sits
upon the bench*) Now produce your prisoners – here, that
fellow there – set him up. [CONSTABLE *brings first prisoner to*   30
the dock] Mr Constable, what have you to say against this
man?

CONSTABLE

I have nothing to say against him, an't please ye.

BALANCE

No? What made you bring him hither?

CONSTABLE

I don't know, an't please your worship.   35

SCRUPLE

Did not the contents of your warrant direct you what sort of
men to take up?

CONSTABLE

I can't tell, an't please ye, I can't read.

---

20 *with a witness* with a vengeance   37 *take up* seize by legal authority

---

28 *sit by me.* 'In order that the proceedings' of conscription under the
Impressment Acts 'might be deemed *Civil* and not Military, the statute
provided that no Justice of the Peace having any military office or
employment . . . should execute the Act' (Clode, op. cit., II, 15). As Hill
has noticed, the physical presence of Plume on the bench helps to point
to the possible abuses inherent in obedience to the letter and not the
spirit of the Acts (J. Burton Hill, op cit., I, 203)

SCRUPLE

A very pretty constable truly! I find we have no business
here.   40

KITE

May it please the worshipful bench, I desire to be heard in
this case, as being counsel for the Queen.

BALANCE

Come, Sergeant, you shall be heard, since nobody else will
speak; we won't come here for nothing.

KITE

This man is but one man, the country may spare him and   45
the army wants him; besides, he's cut out by nature for a
grenadier: he's five foot ten inches high, he shall box,
wrestle, or dance the Cheshire Round with any man in the
county, he gets drunk every sabbath-day, and he beats his
wife.   50

WIFE

You lie, sirrah, you lie, an't please your worship, he's the
best-natured, pains-taking man in the parish, witness my
five poor children.

SCRUPLE

A wife! And five children! You, Constable, you rogue, how
durst you impress a man that has a wife and five children?   55

SCALE

Discharge him, discharge him.

BALANCE

Hold, gentlemen. – Hark'ee, friend, how do you maintain
your wife and five children?

KITE

They live upon wild fowl and venison, sir; the husband
keeps a gun, and kills all the hares and partridges within   60
five mile round.

BALANCE

A gun! Nay, if he be so good at gunning he shall have
enough on't – he may be of use against the French, for he
shoots flying to be sure.

SCRUPLE

But his wife and children, Mr Balance!   65

WIFE

Aye, aye, that's the reason you would send him away: you

42 *counsel* punning on 'sergeant': barrister
58 *five* Q2 (not in Q1)
59 s.p. KITE Ed. (PLUME Q)

know I have a child every year, and you're afraid they
should come upon the parish at last.

PLUME

Look'ee there, gentlemen, the honest woman has spoke it at
once; the parish had better maintain five children this year   70
than six or seven the next; that fellow upon his high feeding
may get you two or three beggars at a birth.

WIFE

Look'ee, Mr Captain, the parish shall get nothing by sending
him away, for I won't lose my teeming-time if there be a
man left in the parish.   75

BALANCE

Send that woman to the house of correction – and the man –

KITE

I'll take care o'him, if you please.   *Takes him down*

SCALE

Here, you Constable, the next: set up that black-faced
fellow, he has a gunpowder look; [CONSTABLE *sets up* SECOND
PRISONER] what can you say against this man, Constable?   80

CONSTABLE

Nothing, but that he's a very honest man.

PLUME

Pray, gentlemen, let me have one honest man in my company for the novelty's sake.

BALANCE

What are you, friend?

SECOND PRISONER

A collier, I work in the coal-pits.   85

SCRUPLE

Look'ee, gentlemen, this fellow has a trade, and the Act of
Parliament here expresses, that we are to impress no man
that has any visible means of a livelihood.

KITE

May it please your worships, this man has no visible means
of a livelihood, for he works underground.   90

PLUME

Well said, Kite – Besides, the army wants miners.

BALANCE

Right! And had we an order of government for't, we could
raise you in this and the neighbouring county of Stafford
five hundred colliers that would run you underground like

77 s.d. *him* Q2 (*the man* Q1)
85 s.p. SECOND PRISONER Ed. (MOB Q)

moles, and do more service in a siege that all the miners in   95
the army.

SCRUPLE

Well, friend, what have you to say for yourself?

SECOND PRISONER

I'm married.

KITE

Lack-a-day, so am I.

SECOND PRISONER

Here's my wife, poor woman.   100

BALANCE

Are you married, good woman?

WOMAN

I'm married in conscience.

KITE

May it please your worship, she's with child in conscience.

SCALE

Who married you, mistress?

WOMAN

My husband – we agreed that I should call him husband to   105
avoid passing for a whore, and that he should call me wife to
shun going for a soldier.

SCRUPLE

A very pretty couple! Pray, Captain, will you take 'em both?

PLUME

What say you, Mr Kite – will you take care of the woman?

KITE

Yes, sir, she shall go with us to the seaside and there if she   110
has a mind to drown herself we'll take care that nobody
shall hinder her. [*Takes down* SECOND PRISONER]

BALANCE

Here, Constable, bring in my man.   *Exit* CONSTABLE
Now, Captain, I'll fit you with a man such as you ne'er listed
in your life.   115

Enter CONSTABLE *and* SILVIA

Oh my friend Pinch, I'm very glad to see you.

SILVIA

Well, sir, and what then?

SCALE

What then! Is that your respect to the bench?

SILVIA

Sir, I don't care a farthing for you nor your bench neither.

SCRUPLE

Look'ee, gentlemen, that's enough, he's a very impudent   120
fellow, and fit for a soldier.

SCALE

A notorious rogue, I say, and very fit for a soldier.

CONSTABLE

A whoremaster, I say, and therefore fit to go.

BALANCE

What think you, Captain?

PLUME

I think he's a very pretty fellow, and therefore fit to serve.   125

SILVIA

Me for a soldier! Send your own lazy, lubberly sons at home,
fellows that hazard their necks every day in pursuit of a fox,
yet dare not peep abroad to look an enemy in the face.

CONSTABLE

May it please your worships, I have a woman at the door to
swear a rape against this rogue.   130

SILVIA

Is it your wife or daughter, booby? I ravished 'em both
yesterday.

BALANCE

Pray, Captain, read the Articles of War, we'll see him listed
immediately.

PLUME (*Reads*)

'Articles of War against Mutiny and Desertion . . .'   135

SILVIA

Hold, sir. – Once more, gentlemen, have a care what you do,
for you shall severely smart for any violence you offer to me;
and you, Mr Balance, I speak to you particularly, you shall
heartily repent it.

PLUME

Look'ee, young spark, say but one word more and I'll build   140
a horse for you as high as the ceiling, and make you ride the
most tiresome journey that ever you made in your life.

SILVIA

You have made a fine speech, good Captain Huffcap, but you

---

135 PLUME (*Reads*)/*Articles* . . . Ed. (PLUME *reads Articles of War
against Mutiny and Desertion* Q)
143 *Huffcap* swashbuckler

---

141 *horse* 'Riding the great horse', or timber mare, was a military punishment. The soldier was made to sit astride raised boards set at an acute
angle, often with muskets tied to his legs (Scouller, p. 268).

had better be quiet, I shall find a way to cool your courage.

PLUME

Pray, gentlemen, don't mind him, he's distracted.   145

SILVIA

'Tis false – I'm descended of as good a family as any in your county, my father is as good a man as any upon your bench, and I am heir to twelve hundred pound a year.

BALANCE

He's certainly mad – pray, Captain, read the Articles of War.

SILVIA

Hold, once more. – Pray, Mr Balance, to you I speak: sup-   150
pose I were your child, would you use me at this rate?

BALANCE

No, faith, were you mine, I would send you to Bedlam first, and into the army afterwards.

SILVIA

But consider my father, sir, he's as good, as generous, as brave, as just a man as ever served his country; I'm his only   155
child, perhaps the loss of me may break his heart.

BALANCE

He's a very great fool if it does. Captain, if you don't list him this minute I'll leave the court.

PLUME

Kite, do you distribute the levy-money to the men whilst I read.   160

KITE

Aye, sir, – silence, gentlemen.

PLUME *reads the Articles of War*

BALANCE

Very well; now, Captain, let me beg the favour of you not to discharge this fellow upon any account whatsoever. – Bring in the rest.

CONSTABLE

There are no more, an't please your worship.   165

BALANCE

No more! There were five two hours ago.

SILVIA

'Tis true, sir, but this rogue of a constable let the rest escape for a bribe of eleven shillings a man, because he said that the Act allows him but ten, so the odd shilling was clear gains.

---

144 *cool . . . courage* proverbial.Tilley, C716
152 *Bedlam* lunatic asylum in London
161 s.d. *the Articles of War* see Appendix 4

ALL JUSTICES

How!   170

SILVIA

Gentlemen, he offered to let me get away for two guineas,
but I had not so much about me. – This is truth, and I'm
ready to swear it.

KITE

And I'll swear it, give me the book, 'tis for the good of the
service.   175

SECOND PRISONER

May it please your worship, I gave him half a crown to say
that I was an honest man, – but now since that your worships have made me a rogue, I hope I shall have my money
again.

BALANCE

'Tis my opinion that this constable be put into the captain's   180
hands, and if his friends don't bring four good men for his
ransom by tomorrow night – Captain, you shall carry him to
Flanders.

SCALE, SCRUPLE

Agreed, agreed.

PLUME

Mr Kite, take the constable into custody.   185

KITE

Aye, aye, sir. – (*To the* CONSTABLE) Will you please to have
your office taken from you, or will you handsomely lay
down your staff as your betters have done before you?

> *The* CONSTABLE *drops his staff*

BALANCE

Come, gentlemen, there needs no great ceremony in adjourn-
ing this court; – Captain, you shall dine with me.   190

KITE

Come Mr Militia Sergeant, I shall silence you now I
believe, without your taking the law of me.

> *Exeunt omnes*

---

177 *but now since* Q2 (and now Q1)

187–8 *lay down your staff*. The phrase was used for the resignation of
     ministers of state.

[Act V], Scene vi

The Fields
Enter BRAZEN *leading in* LUCY *masked*

BRAZEN

The boat is just below here.

Enter WORTHY *with a case of pistols under his arm*

WORTHY

Here, sir, take your choice.

Going between 'em, and offering them

BRAZEN

What! Pistols! Are they charged, my dear?

WORTHY

With a brace of bullets each.

BRAZEN

But I'm a foot-officer, my dear, and never use pistols, the   5
sword is my way – and I won't be put out of my road to
please any man.

WORTHY

Nor I neither, so have at you.   *Cocks one pistol*

BRAZEN

Look'ee, my dear, I don't care for pistols; – pray oblige me
and let us have a bout at sharps; damn't there's no parrying   10
these bullets.

WORTHY

Sir, if you han't your belly full of these, the swords shall
come in for second course.

BRAZEN

Why then fire and fury! I have eaten smoke from the mouth
of a cannon, sir, don't think I fear powder, for I live upon't.   15
Let me see. (*Takes one*) And now, sir, how many paces
distant shall we fire?

WORTHY

Fire you when you please, I'll reserve my shot till I be sure
of you.

BRAZEN

Come, where's your cloak?   20

0.1–0.2 *The Fields/Enter . . . masked* Q2 ([SCENE] *changes to the
Fields*, BRAZEN *leading in* LUCY *masked* Q1)
1 s.d. *arm* Q2 (*arm, parts* BRAZEN *and* LUCY Q1)
2 s.d. *Going . . . them* Q2 (*Offering the pistols* Q1)
10 *sharps* duelling swords
16 s.d. *one* Q2 (*a pistol* Q1)

WORTHY

Cloak! What d'ye mean?

BRAZEN

To fight upon, I always fight upon a cloak, 'tis our way
abroad.

LUCY

Come, gentlemen, I'll end the strife.   *Unmasks*

WORTHY

Lucy! Take her.   25

BRAZEN

The devil take me if I do – Huzza! (*Fires his pistol*) D'ye
hear, d'ye hear, you plaguey harridan, how those bullets
whistle, suppose they had been lodged in my gizzard
now? –

LUCY

Pray, sir, pardon me.   30

BRAZEN

I can't tell, child, till I know whether my money be safe.
(*Searching his pockets*) Yes, yes, I do pardon you, – but if I
had you in the Rose Tavern, Covent Garden, with three or
four hearty rakes, and three or four smart napkins, I would
tell you another story, my dear.   *Exit*   35

WORTHY

And was Melinda privy to this?

LUCY

No, sir; she wrote her name upon a piece of paper at the
fortune-teller's last night, which I put in my pocket, and
so writ above it to the captain.

WORTHY

And how came Melinda's journey put off?   40

LUCY

At the town's end she met Mr Balance's steward, who told
her that Mrs Silvia was gone from her father's, and nobody
could tell whither.

WORTHY

Silvia gone from her father's! This will be news to Plume.
Go home, and tell your lady how near I was being shot for   45
her.   *Exeunt*

24 s.d. *Unmasks* Q2 (*Pulls off her mask* Q1)
34 *napkins* probably slang for whores

---

33 *Rose Tavern, Covent Garden.* In Russell Street, adjoining the Drury
Lane Theatre, 'a favourite place of resort after the play', also, 'a noted
haunt of bad characters, especially those of the female sex' (Ewald).

[Act V], Scene vii
[BALANCE's *house*]
Enter BALANCE *with a napkin in his hand, as risen from dinner, and* STEWARD

STEWARD

We did not miss her till the evening, sir, and then searching for her in the chamber that was my young master's, we found her clothes there, but the suit that your son left in the press when he went to London was gone.

BALANCE

The white, trimmed with silver!   5

STEWARD

The same.

BALANCE

You han't told that circumstance to anybody?

STEWARD

To none but your worship.

BALANCE

And be sure you don't. Go into the dining-room, and tell Captain Plume that I beg to speak with him.   10

STEWARD

I shall.   *Exit*

BALANCE

Was ever man so imposed upon? I had her promise indeed that she should never dispose of herself without my consent. – I have consented with a witness, given her away as my act and deed – and this, I warrant, the captain thinks will pass;   15
no, I shall never pardon him the villainy, first of robbing me of my daughter, and then the mean opinion he must have of me to think that I could be so wretchedly imposed upon; her extravagant passion might encourage her in the attempt, but the contrivance must be his – I'll know the truth presently.   20

Enter PLUME

Pray, Captain, what have you done with your young gentleman soldier?

PLUME

He's at my quarters, I suppose, with the rest of my men.

BALANCE

Does he keep company with the common soldiers?

0.3 s.d. BALANCE's *house* Ed. (not in Q)
0.1 s.d. *and* STEWARD Q2 (*talking with his* STEWARD Q1)

PLUME

No, he's generally with me.   25

BALANCE

He lies with you, I presume?

PLUME

No, faith, – I offered him part of my bed, but the young
rogue fell in love with Rose, and has lain with her, I think,
since he came to town.

BALANCE

So that between you both, Rose has been finely managed.   30

PLUME

Upon my honour, sir, she had no harm from me.

BALANCE

All's safe, I find. – Now, Captain, you must know that the
young fellow's impudence in court was well grounded; he
said I should heartily repent his being listed, and so I do
from my soul.   35

PLUME

Aye! For what reason?

BALANCE

Because he is no less than what he said he was, born of as
good a family as any in this county, and is heir to twelve
hundred pound a year.

PLUME

I'm very glad to hear it, for I wanted but a man of that   40
quality to make my company a perfect representative of the
whole commons of England.

BALANCE

Won't you discharge him?

PLUME

Not under a hundred pound sterling.

BALANCE

You shall have it, for his father is my intimate friend.   45

PLUME

Then you shall have him for nothing.

BALANCE

Nay, sir, you shall have your price.

PLUME

Not a penny, sir; I value an obligation to you much above a
hundred pound.

BALANCE

Perhaps, sir, you shan't repent your generosity. – Will you 50

34 *said I* Q2 (said that I Q1)   34 *so* Q2 (not in Q1)

please to write his discharge in my pocket-book? (*Gives his book*) In the meantime we'll send for the gentleman. Who waits there?

Enter SERVANT

Go to the captain's lodgings and inquire for Mr Wilful; tell him his captain wants him here immediately. 55

SERVANT

Sir, the gentleman's below at the door inquiring for the captain.

PLUME

Bid him come up – here's the discharge, sir.

BALANCE

Sir, I thank you. – (*Aside*) 'Tis plain he had no hand in't.

Enter SILVIA

SILVIA

I think, Captain, you might have used me better, than to 60 leave me yonder among your swearing, drunken crew; and you, Mr Justice, might have been so civil as to have invited me to dinner, for I have eaten with as good a man as your worship.

PLUME

Sir, you must charge our want of respect upon our ignorance 65 of your quality – but now you're at liberty – I have discharged you.

SILVIA

Discharged me!

BALANCE

Yes, sir, and you must once more go home to your father.

SILVIA

My father! Then I'm discovered! Oh sir, (*kneeling*) I expect 70 no pardon.

BALANCE

Pardon! No, no, child; your crime shall be your punishment; here, Captain, I deliver her over to the conjugal power for her chastisement; since she will be a wife, be you a husband, a very husband: when she tells you of her love, upbraid her 75 with her folly; be modishly ungrateful, because she has been unfashionably kind; and use her worse than you would anybody else, because you can't use her so well as she deserves.

PLUME

And are you Silvia in good earnest? 80

SILVIA

Earnest! I have gone too far to make it a jest, sir.

PLUME

And do you give her to me in good earnest?

BALANCE

If you please to take her, sir.

PLUME

Why then I have saved my legs and arms, and lost my
liberty; secure from wounds, I'm prepared for the gout;   85
farewell subsistence and welcome taxes. – Sir, my liberty
and hopes of being a general are much dearer to me than
your twelve hundred pound a year – but to your love,
madam, I resign my freedom, and to your beauty my
ambition – greater in obeying at your feet, than commanding   90
at the head of an army.

Enter WORTHY

WORTHY

I'm sorry to hear, Mr Balance, that your daughter is lost.

BALANCE

So am not I, sir, since an honest gentleman has found her.

Enter MELINDA

MELINDA

Pray, Mr Balance, what's become of my cousin Silvia?

BALANCE

Your cousin Silvia is talking yonder with your cousin Plume.   95

MELINDA ⎫
WORTHY ⎬
How!   ⎭

SILVIA

Do you think it strange, cousin, that a woman should change?
But, I hope, you'll excuse a change that has proceeded from
constancy; I altered my outside because I was the same
within, and only laid by the woman to make sure of my man;   100
that's my history.

MELINDA

Your history is a little romantic, cousin, but since success has
crowned your adventures you will have the world o' your
side, and I shall be willing to go with the tide, provided you
pardon an injury I offered you in the letter to your father.   105

83 s.p. BALANCE Q1 (SILVIA Q2)

---

97 *that a woman should change.* cf. *Æneid*, IV, 569: *Varium et mutabile
semper fœmina.* Also, proverbial. Tilley, W674, W698.

PLUME

That injury, madam, was done to me, and the reparation I
expect shall be made to my friend; make Mr Worthy happy,
and I shall be satisfied.

MELINDA

A good example, sir, will go a great way – when my cousin is
pleased to surrender, 'tis probable I shan't hold out much   110
longer.

Enter BRAZEN

BRAZEN

Gentlemen, I am yours – madam, I am not yours.

MELINDA

I'm glad on't, sir.

BRAZEN

So am I. – You have got a pretty house here, Mr Laconic.

BALANCE

'Tis time to right all mistakes – my name, sir, is Balance.   115

BRAZEN

Balance! Sir, I'm your most obedient. – I know your whole
generation – had not you an uncle that was governor of the
Leeward Islands some years ago?

BALANCE

Did you know him?

BRAZEN

Intimately, sir – he played at billiards to a miracle; you had   120
a brother, too, that was captain of a fireship – poor Dick – he
had the most engaging way with him – of making punch, –
and then his cabin was so neat – but his boy Jack was the most
comical bastard – ha, ha, ha, ha, a pickled dog, I shall never
forget him.   125

PLUME

Well, Captain, are you fixed in your project yet? Are you
still for the privateer?

BRAZEN

No, no, I had enough of a privateer just now, I had like to
have been picked up by a cruiser under false colours, and a
French picaroon for aught I know.   130

PLUME

But have you got your recruits, my dear?

BRAZEN

Not a stick, my dear.

124 *pickled dog* arch or waggish fellow

130 *French picaroon* pirate or privateer, i.e., whore with the 'French
    disease', syphilis

PLUME

Probably I shall furnish you.

Enter ROSE *and* BULLOCK

ROSE

Captain, Captain, I have got loose once more, and have
persuaded my sweetheart Cartwheel to go with us, but you   135
must promise not to part with me again.

SILVIA

I find Mrs Rose has not been pleased with her bedfellow.

ROSE

Bedfellow! I don't know whether I had a bedfellow or not.

SILVIA

Don't be in a passion, child, I was as little pleased with your
company as you could be with mine.   140

BULLOCK

Pray, sir, dunna be offended at my sister, she's something
underbred – but if you please I'll lie with you in her stead.

PLUME

I have promised, madam, to provide for this girl; now will
you be pleased to let her wait upon you, or shall I take care
of her?   145

SILVIA

She shall be my charge, sir, you may find it business enough
to take care of me.

BULLOCK

Aye, and of me, Captain, for wauns! if ever you lift your
hand against me, I'll desert.

PLUME

Captain Brazen shall take care o' that. – My dear, instead of   150
the twenty thousand pound you talked of, you shall have the
twenty brave recruits that I have raised, at the rate they
cost me. – My commission I lay down to be taken up by
some braver fellow, that has more merit and less good
fortune, whilst I endeavour by the example of this worthy   155
gentleman to serve my Queen and country at home.

> With some regret I quit the active field,
> Where glory full reward for life does yield;
> But the recruiting trade, with all its train
> Of lasting plague, fatigue, and endless pain,   160
> I gladly quit, with my fair spouse to stay,
> And raise recruits the matrimonial way.

Exeunt

162.1 s.d. *Exeunt* Q2 (not in Q1)

EPILOGUE

All ladies and gentlemen that are willing to see the comedy
called *The Recruiting Officer*, let them repair tomorrow night by
six o'clock to the sign of the Theatre Royal in Drury Lane, and
they shall be kindly entertained –

> We scorn the vulgar ways to bid you come,　　　　　5
> Whole Europe now obeys the call of drum.
> The soldier, not the poet, here appears,
> And beats up for a corps of volunteers;
> He finds that music chiefly does delight ye,
> And therefore chooses music to invite ye.　　　　　10

Beat the *Grenadier March* – Row, row, tow! – Gentlemen,
this piece of music, called *An Overture to a Battle*, was composed by a famous Italian master, and was performed with
wonderful success, at the great operas of Vigo, Schellenberg,
and Blenheim; it came off with the applause of all Europe,　　15
excepting France; the French found it a little too rough for
their *delicatesse*.

> Some that have acted on those glorious stages,
> Are here to witness to succeeding ages
> That no music like the *Grenadier's* engages.　　　　20

Ladies, we must own that this music of ours is not altogether
so soft as Bononcini's, yet we dare affirm, that it has laid more

1–4 Cf. Kite's announcement, I.i, 1–7; this also echoes contemporary
advertisements for concerts.

9–37 The past year had seen the growth of a passionate demand for
Italianate opera.

14 *Vigo, Schellenberg, and Blenheim*. The three proudest Allied victories in
the current war, to this time. On 12 October 1702 Sir George Rooke's
fleet, assisted by Ormonde's army (cf. note, dedicatory epistle, l. 61),
burnt the Spanish and French shipping in Vigo harbour, sacked the
town, and carried off a gratifying array of booty. Marlborough's costly
victory over the Elector of Bavaria's army at the Schellenbergh Heights on
2 July 1704 was a necessary preliminary to the decisive triumph at
Blenheim on 13 August (see note to II.i, 13).

22 *Bononcini's* Antonio Maria Bononcini (1675–1726), composer of the
music for *Camilla* (originally, *Il Trionfo di Camilla, regina de' Volsci*).
For the Drury Lane production his score had been adapted by Nicolo
Haym, with Stampiglia's libretto translated by Owen Swiney and
Mr Northam (see Nicoll, p. 274). It was performed on 30 March and
6 April, two days before Farquhar's opening night, and also interrupted
the run of *The Recruiting Officer*, on the 11th.

people asleep than all the *Camillas* in the world; and you'll
condescend to own that it keeps one awake better than any
opera that ever was acted. 25

The *Grenadier March* seems to be a composure excellently
adapted to the genius of the English; for no music was ever
followed so far by us, nor with so much alacrity; and with all
deference to the present subscription, we must say that the
Grenadier March has been subscribed for by the whole Grand 30
Alliance; and we presume to inform the ladies, that it always
has the pre-eminence abroad, and is constantly heard by the
tallest, handsomest men in the whole army. In short, to gratify
the present taste, our author is now adapting some words to
the *Grenadier March*, which he intends to have performed 35
tomorrow, if the lady who is to sing it should not happen to be
sick.

> This he concludes to be the surest way
> To draw you hither, for you'll all obey
> Soft music's call, though you should damn his play. 40

26 *composure* composition
29 *subscription* the arrangement by which the production-costs of
   Camilla were met by public subscription; the people so sub-
   scribing
30–1 *the Grand Alliance* England, the Dutch Republic, the Empire,
   the Spanish supporters of Archduke Charles, and some German
   states in coalition against France
36–7 *if. . . sick* Dixon suggests this is a 'jibe at the temperamentality of
   such prima donnas as Catherine Tofts', an opera singer at Drury
   Lane in 1705–6.

APPENDIX 1

TEXTUAL

(A) *Passages in Q1 deleted in Q2*

Minor Q2 cuts have been noticed in footnotes, and several more substantial passages, notably the song in Act III, scene i, and the entirety of Act V, scene i, retained in the text, being clearly delimited and not distorting their contexts.

(i) First version of part of Silvia-Plume *tête-a-tête*, Act II, scene i, replaced by the present edition's ll. 51–64:

PLUME

Blessings in heaven we should receive in a prostrate posture, let me receive my welcome thus.   *Kneels and kisses her hand*

SILVIA

Pray rise, sir, I'll give you fair quarter.

PLUME

All quarter I despise, the height of conquest is to die at your feet.   *Kissing her hand again*

SILVIA

Well, well, you shall die at my feet, or where you will; but first let me desire you to make your will, perhaps you'll leave me something.

(ii) First version of Silvia-Plume argument over Rose, Act IV, scene i, replaced in the present edition by ll. 56–82:

PLUME

. . . Let her go, I say.

SILVIA

Do you let her go.

PLUME

Entendez vous français, mon petit garçon?

SILVIA

Oui.

PLUME

Si voulez vous donc vous enroller dans ma compagnie, la demoiselle sera à vous.

SILVIA

Avez vous couché avec elle?

PLUME

Non.

SILVIA

Assurement?

PLUME

Ma foi

SILVIA

C'est assez. Je serai votre soldat.

PLUME

La prenez donc. I'll change a woman for a man at any time.

(iii) Devil incident in Act IV, scene ii:

(a) Following Kite's 'Here Tre, Tre, poor Tre, give me the bone, sirrah – ', the present l. 237,

> *He puts his hand under the table,* PLUME *steals to the other side of the table and catches him by the hand*[1]

KITE

Oh! oh! The Devil, the Devil in good earnest, my hand, the Devil, my hand!

> MELINDA *and* LUCY *shriek, and run to a corner of the stage.* KITE *discovers* PLUME *and gets away his hand*

KITE

A plague o' your pincers, he has fixed his nails in my very flesh. Oh! Madam, you put the Devil in such a passion with your scruples, that it has almost cost me my hand.

MELINDA

It has cost us our lives almost – but have you got the name?

KITE

Got it! Aye, madam, I have got it here – I'm sure the blood comes – but there's your name upon that square piece of paper – behold –

(b) Corresponding passage, at Plume and Worthy's entry, ll. 280 ff. (they enter '*laughing*'):

KITE

Aye, you may well laugh, gentlemen, not all the cannon of the French army could have frighted me so much as that gripe you gave me under the table.

PLUME

I think, Mr Doctor, I out-conjured you that bout.

KITE

I was surprised, for I should not have taken a captain for a conjurer.

PLUME

No more than I should a sergeant for a wit.

(B) *Revisions in 'Works', 1728*

Certain revisions which clearly relate to the current prompt-book and may reflect much earlier stage-practice appear in the 6th edition of *The Works of the Late Ingenious Mr George Farquhar*, etc., of 1728. Presumably the changes were initiated by William Rufus Chetwood, who supplied the biography of the author which first appeared in

---

[1] In Q1, s.d. follows '. . . my hand'; this arrangement is Hunt's.

1728. These revisions do not appear in the editions of the play printed separately till 1736 (the copy, British Museum L.1342.n.27, has 1736 on its title-page though it is catalogued as '1728'), nor in the reprints of *The Comedies of Mr Farquhar* (7th edition, 1736: *The Dramatic Works . . .*). Accordingly, the denotation through the critical notes of 'later C18 editions' means '*Works*, 1728, text and those that follow it'. These changes include, among others:

(i) Act I, scene i: the entry direction has 'Thomas Appletree, Costar Pearmain *and the Mob*', rather than '*the Mob*'; and in this scene '*Costar*' or '*Cost*' appears as a speech-prefix in place of '*Mob*'. In 'Costar's' third speech, he adds, after 'brimstone': 'Smell Tummas', and the latter replies 'Aye, wauns does it'.

(ii) In Act II, scene iii, the first stage direction has '*Enter* Kite, *with* Costar Pearmain *in one hand and* Thomas Appletree *in the other, drunk*', in place of '*Enter* Kite, *with one of the* Mob *in each hand, drunk*'. The speech-prefixes are *Kite*, *Thomas*, and *Costar*, rather than *Kite*, *1st Mob*, and *2d Mob*.

(iii) At the end of Act II, scene iii, when Costar gives his name, Plume replies: 'Well said, Costar. Born where?' in place of 'Born where?' The last verse of the song is complete, as in the present edition, and is followed by:

PLUME
> Kite, take care of 'em.

Enter KITE

KITE
> Ain't you a couple of pretty fellows now! Here have you complained to the captain, I am to be turned out, and one of you will be sergeant. But in the meantime, march, you sons of whores.
> *Beats 'em off*

(iv) An extra gag appears in Act III, scene i: Rose's 'familiarity' (the present l. 288) becomes 'fam-mam-mil-yararality'.

(v) Act V, scene iv, begins with Plume's saying: 'A baker, a taylor, smith, butcher, carpenters and journeyman shoemakers, in all thirty-nine – I believe . . .'

(C) *Bell's acting edition, 1776*, etc.

John Bell's *British Theatre* volumes appeared first in 1776, with *The Recruiting Officer* in volume IV. The text is 'as written by G. Farquhar, Esq. Distinguishing also the variations of the theatre, as performed at the Theatre-Royal in Drury-Lane. Regulated from the prompt-book, by permission of the managers, by Mr Hopkins, Prompter'. Passages for omission in presentation are marked off with inverted commas, apart from a few omitted silently. The version follows Q2, and all changes introduced in the 1728 edition are present.[2]

Another edition 'marked with the variations in the prompter's book' published in the same year by T. Lowndes was probably essentially similar, as the 1792 edition of Bell's text was to be described as that in use at both theatres, Drury Lane and Covent Garden.

Two minor kinds of changes are introduced throughout: 'queen' becomes 'king', 'Queen Anne' becomes 'King George', and Rose in III.i, 267 is going to London to see 'the king and queen'. Also, 'broad pieces' worth 23s. 6d. in Act II, scene iii, become guineas worth 'one and twenty shillings'.

The following are the cuts or revisions of more than a few words:

I.i: 195–6 cut, 'and pushed it with all my forces'; 248–50 cut, 'her sex . . . in her'; 255 'fifty' becomes 'a hundred'.

I.ii: 49–52 cut, 'Constancy . . . noble sex'.

II.i: 2–7 cut, 'I remember . . . prisoners'.[3]

II.ii: 26–36 cut, 'Besides . . . gravel walks'; 149–50 cut, 'the decorum . . . us'.

II.iii: the end, instead of 'But in the meantime, march, you sons of whores', Kite says:

> . . . Which of you is to have my halberd?

BOTH REC [RUITS]
> I.

KITE
> So you shall – in your guts –
> March, you sons of whores.

Beats 'em off

III.i: 4–5 cut, 'a maggot fills their heads'; 111 added, after 'say it'

WORTHY
> How came you so qualified?

115 cut, 'who liking . . . page'; 160–1 'fight' and 'Irish' become 'sea-fight' and 'wild Irish'; 162–3 speech assigned to

---

[2] The edition of Bell's text inspected is that of 1792, but the presence of the listed variants in the 1776 edition has been kindly checked by Professor H. F. Brooks. A prompt-book of this era is included in volume 8 of a collection of thirty-eight Covent Garden prompt-books represented in microfilm at the University of North Carolina.

[3] So, 1776. In 1792 the remaining words of the speech, 'Ad's my life [for 'odsmylife] . . . soldier', were also marked for omission; they may have been intended to be in 1776, and not marked as such by accident.

Kite; 175–9 cut, 'I never . . . world'; 180–3 cut 'Cupid . . .
lamely'; 196–203 cut, 'I have . . . moment'.

III.ii: 15–26 cut, 'Madam . . . ourselves'.

IV.i: 8–9 cut, 'this genteel . . . followers'; 122–33 'the women . . .
bear it'; 138–45 cut, 'You must . . . else'; 188–207 cut, 'You're . . .
together'; 285–7 cut, 'there's . . . conduct'.

IV.ii: 19–195 cut, from Smith's entry to just before Melinda's
entry (i.e., to ' 'tis Madam Melinda'); 308 ff. added, after 'aye or
no'.

KITE
Certainly.
BRAZEN
Gadso, aye –
KITE
– Or no – but I must . . .

V.i: as in Q2, cut completely.

V.ii: 3–15 cut, 'they expose . . . This'; 60–1 cut, '*bien* . . . button'.

V.iii: 12–15 cut, 'which . . . abroad'.

V.iv: 1–3 cut, 'I believe . . . mine'; 19–37 cut, 'now, my dear . . .
Agreed'.

V.vi: scene cut completely.

V.vii: 126–30 cut, 'Well . . . know'.

APPENDIX 2

SONGS

FARQUHAR'S SONG 'Come, fair one, be kind' in Act III, scene i, set to music by Richard Leveridge, was published separately on a single folio sheet as 'A SONG *Set by* Mr Leveridge *Sung by* Mr Wilks *in the Comedy call'd the* Recruiting Officer'.[1] The tune printed below from this sheet was later used by John Gay as Air XV in *The Beggar's Opera* (1728).

Act II, scene iii begins and ends with verses and a chorus, which would appear later in a song called 'The Recruiting Officer: or, The Merry Volunteers', published in Thomas Durfey's *Wit and Mirth: or Pills to Purge Melancholy* (1719–20), V, 319–21. It is not known whether the words, as a whole, were written before Farquhar's play or soon after, or by whom. The tune, called 'Over the hills and far away', was printed in 1706 by Thomas Durfey as the tune for his song 'Jockey's Lamentation' (*Pills* [1706], IV, 99). It became very popular and also appeared in *The Beggar's Opera*.[2] Whoever wrote the words, they are of sufficient relevance to reprint entire.

John Genest has preserved the memory of an incident when news reached Bath of Prince Eugene's victory at Turin on 7 September 1706, after an epic two months' march from Lake Garda, which helps to confirm the basically patriotic tendency of the verses within the play, and of the play itself.

On Sep. 16 1706 the Recruiting Officer was acted at Bath – several persons of quality were present – the news of the victory gained by the Duke of Savoy and Prince Eugene, reached Bath that day – Estcourt [playing Kite] added to the song in the 2d. act –

> The noble Captain Prince Eugene
> Has beat French, Orleans and Marsin,
> And march'd up and reliev'd Turin,
> – Over the hills and far away.[3]

Plume's snatch of song as he enters near the end of Act III, scene i, is the refrain of a song first written by Martin Parker in 1634,

[1] Also in the April 1706 issue of *The Monthly Mask of Vocal Music*, not seen, but advertised in *The Daily Courant*, 11 April 1706.
[2] Claude M. Simpson, *The British Broadside and its Music* (New Brunswick, 1966), pp. 561–3.
[3] *Some Account of the English Stage from the Restoration in 1660 to 1830* [Bath, 1832], II, 340.

called 'The Milke-maids Life', to a tune generally known as 'The Milkmaids', 'The Merry Milkmaids', or 'The Milking Pail'. The words were reworked in 1694 by Thomas Durfey for his play *Don Quixote*, Part II with new music supplied by John Eccles. It is presumably this new tune which Plume used, but both are provided.[4]

The 'Grenadier[s'] March' which opens and closes the play is doubtless the tune which first appeared in *A Collection of the Newest and Choicest Songs*, 1683.

The Recruiting Officer: Or,
The Merry Volunteers: Being
an Excellent New Copy of Verses
upon raising Recruits.

Hark! now the drums beat up again,
For all true soldiers gentlemen,
Then let us list, and march I say,
Over the hills and far away;
Over the hills and o'er the main,
To Flanders, Portugal and Spain,
Queen Anne commands, and we'll obey,
  Over the hills and far away.

All gentlemen that have a mind,
To serve the queen that's good and kind;
Come list and enter into pay,
Then o'er the hills and far away;
  Over the hills, &c.

Here's forty shillings on the drum,
For those that volunteers do come,
With shirts, and clothes, and present pay,
When o'er the hills and far away;
  Over the hills, &c.

Hear that brave boys, and let us go,
Or else we shall be prest you know;
Then list and enter into pay,
And o'er the hills and far away,
  Over the hills, &c.

The constables they search about,
To find such brisk young fellows out;
Then let's be volunteers I say,
Over the hills and far away;
  Over the hills, &c.

[4] Simpson, pp. 490–3.

Since now the French so low are brought,
And wealth and honour's to be got,
Who then behind would sneaking stay?
When o'er the hills and far away;
   Over the hills, &c.

No more from sound of drum retreat,
While Marlborough and Gallaway beat
The French and Spaniards every day,
When over the hills and far away;
   Over the hills, &c.

He that is forced to go and fight,
Will never get true honour by't,
While volunteers shall win the day,
When o'er the hills and far away;
   Over the hills, &c.

What tho' our friends our absence mourn,
We all with honour shall return;
And then we'll sing both night and day,
Over the hills and far away;
   Over the hills, &c.

The prentice Tom he may refuse,
To wipe his angry master's shoes;
For then he's free to sing and play,
Over the hills and far away;
   Over the hills, &c.

Over rivers, bogs, and springs,
We all shall live as great as kings,
And plunder get both night and day,
When over the hills and far away,
   Over the hills, &c.

We then shall lead more happy lives,
By getting rid of brats and wives,
That scold on both night and day,
When o'er the hills and far away:
   Over the hills, &c.

Come on then boys and you shall see,
We every one shall captains be,
To whore and rant as well as they,
When o'er the hills and far away:
   Over the hills, &c.

For if we go 'tis one to ten,
But we return all gentlemen,
All gentlemen as well as they,
When o'er the hills and far away:
   Over the hills, &c.

(1) 'Come, fair one, be kind'.

(2) 'Over the hills and far away,' from Simpson, op. cit., p. 562.

(3a) The Milkmaids, first tune.

(3b) The Milkmaids, Eccles' tune.

(4) Grenadier March

Based on the music provided in the *Revels* edition of *The Recruiting Officer* (Manchester University Press) by kind permission of the editor, Professor Peter Dixon.

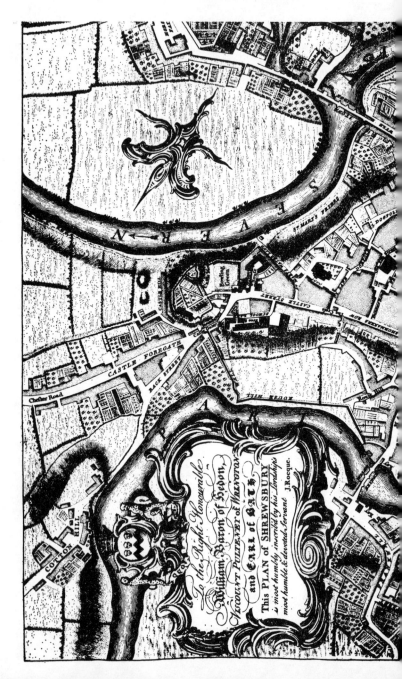

Published by J. Cooper according to an Act of Parliament 1756.

APPENDIX 4

ARTICLES OF WAR AGAINST MUTINY AND DESERTION

Article XIV
No man shall presume so far as to raise or cause the least Mutiny or Sedition in the Army, upon Pain of Death. And if any number of Soldiers shall presume to assemble to take Counsel amongst themselves for the demanding their Pay, or shall at any time demand their Pay in a Mutinous manner, any Inferior Officers accessory thereunto, shall suffer Death for it, as the Heads and Ringleaders of such Mutinous and Seditious Meetings; And the Soldiers shall be punished with Death. And if any Captain, being privy thereunto shall not suppress the same, or complain of it, he shall likewise be punished with Death.

Article XV
No Officer or Soldier shall utter any Words tending to Sedition or Mutiny, upon Pain of Death.
   And whosoever shall hear any Mutinous or Seditious Words spoken, and shall not with all possible speed reveal the same to his Superior Officers, shall likewise be punished with Death.

Article XVI
If any Inferior Officer or Soldier shall refuse to obey his Superior Officer, he shall be punished with Death.

Article XVII
If any Officer or Soldier shall presume to resist any Officer in the Execution of his Office, or shall strike, or lift up his hand to strike, or shall draw, or lift up any Weapon against his Superior Officer upon any Pretence whatsoever, he shall suffer Death.

Article XXII
When any March is to be made, every Man who is sworn shall follow his Colours; and whoever shall without leave stay behind, or depart above a Mile from the Camp, or out of the Army without Licence, shall die for it.

143

Article XXIII

All Officers or Soldiers that shall desert either in the Field, upon a March, in Quarters, or in Garrison, shall Die for it; and all Soldiers shall be reputed and suffer as Deserters, who shall be found a Mile from their Garison or Camp without leave from the Officer Commanding in Chief.

Article XXIV

No Officer or Soldier shall leave his Colours, and List himself into any other Regiment, Troop or Company, without a Discharge from the Commander in Chief of the Regiment, Troop or Company, in which he last served, upon pain of being reputed a Deserter, and suffering Death for it; and in case any Officer shall Receive, or Entertain any Non-Commission Officer or Soldier, who shall have so Deserted or left his Colours without a Discharge, such Officer shall be immediately Cashiered.

From *Rules and Articles for the better Government of Her Majesties Land-Forces in the Low-Countries, and Parts beyond the Seas* (1702), 9-13, all in black letter (O: Vet A4f. 1286). The articles to be read are Nos XIV and XXIII, omitting the passages in No. XIV about 'Inferior Officers' and 'Captains'.

APPENDIX 5

MILITARY PAY

Pay was divided into 'subsistence', intended to be paid at regular intervals in advance, and 'arrears' for officers ('off-reckonings' for other ranks), which were supposed to be distributed at the end of each year after deductions for necessary expenses (R.E. Scouller, *The Armies of Queen Anne*, Oxford: Clarendon Press, 1966, pp. 127–8). Officers might also enjoy various allowances and perquisites.

Each regiment's pay was calculated according to the number of officers and men on the current muster-roll, as determined at musters normally held, at home, every two months. It was issued in bulk to the colonel and administered by his 'agent', the regimental paymaster and clerk.

In practice this system was notoriously unreliable and prone to abuse through official juggling, perquisite-taking or downright dishonesty, at every level.

The State Treasury often had insufficient cash, so that some regiments either were paid in tallies, which could only be converted into cash at a discount – often 30% but sometimes worse – or were not paid at all for years at a time. 'Arrears' (IV.ii,43) could thus have a second, more sinister meaning. Despite the harsh penalties threatened for organising them, 'petitions' from soldiers to Parliament, or any other authority, appealing for the issue of long-overdue pay were numerous, though they seem to have had nuisance value only (Scouller, pp. 131–3, 279; see I.i,84.).

The sums allowed for private soldiers' off-reckonings reached the regiments only after various functionaries and institutions had taken their cut; and any residue, after further rake-offs and payments of expenses, was either pre-empted by the colonel or divided between himself and his senior officers. Hence, from a nominal 8 pence a day, foot-soldiers depended upon subsistence payments of about 3 shillings a week, sometimes less.

Gross pay before deductions for captains of foot was calculated at 10 shillings a day (8 shillings plus 2 shillings for three servants) (cf. II.ii, 24–6), and for lieutenants it was 4 shillings, plus 8 pence for one

145

servant (Scouller, p. 377). (There were 12 pence to the shilling and 20 shillings to the pound sterling.)

Despite efforts to prevent and penalise false musters, the authorities themselves sanctioned the inclusion of a certain number of imaginary men. The enlistment of children, 'absent upon furlough', served as a way of providing a benefit for dead officers' families, though only two 'widows' men' were supposed to be allowed for each regiment (cf. Kite's enlisting of Plume's bastard child, I.i,122–5; though this can be construed as a bribe for Kite himself, for owning parentage, rather than a benefit for the child.) Officers received financial allowances for a set number of servants, depending on rank; and 'custom' permitted them to count these as 'additional personal pay', with their actual servants being mustered and paid as soldiers (Scouller, pp. 144–5; cf. IV.ii,52). Other nominal men ('faggots') were added on to provide for various special expenses, fees and perquisites; and the names of those who had died, deserted or been discharged were often left on the roll by dishonest officers and agents.

Field officers (of the rank of brigadier and above) 'invariably had a company and regiment in their name for which they also drew pay, and any perquisites for which that appointment made them eligible', leaving the duties to others (Scouller, p. 127; cf. III.ii.166–7).

The rank of 'Captain of the Forges to the Grand Train of Artillery', which Kite promises to the smith, does not seem to have formally existed, but the 10 shillings a day he mentions is plausible (IV.ii,50–2), unlike the smith's chances. A captain of artillery would have received £60 a year, plus 10 shillings a day while accompanying the train (Scouller, p. 180).

A Surgeon-General to the Forces would receive 'only 10 shillings a day' rather than the £500 Kite promises the butcher (IV.ii,168); but he could make higher profits from supplying medicines than the lesser surgeons could. Scouller mentions that 'it was not necessary for a doctor to be professionally qualified to obtain employment in the army' (p.236).

The position of the agent gave him splendid opportunities for profit: 'By and large, these agents were probably the biggest rascals living off soldier-men in an age of very keen competition' (Scouller, p. 135; cf. IV.ii,46–7). The agent for Farquhar's regiment, Thomas Southerne the dramatist, made his fortune.

Recruiting was an especially expensive time for a regiment and financially perilous for the more junior officers directly involved. All levy money had to be paid by them 'on the spot'; and if the recipients succeeded in deserting before their first muster, the officers themselves would be held liable for it, and for other disbursements. Some expenses they would have had to pay out of their own pockets, in the uncertain hope of being reimbursed. Farquhar's experience – being forced by debts to sell his commission – was not an unusual one for conscientious and honest men (Scouller, pp. 118–19).